PRAISE FOR
STOP ROBBING PETER TO PAY PAUL

Stop Robbing Peter to Pay Paul was written for people from all walks of life. Its worldwide impact has been life changing. Here's what others have to say...

"In **Stop Robbing Peter to Pay Paul**, Vicky Spring Love presents one of the most profound, yet simple approaches to this essential subject.... I encourage anyone who wants to have a fundamental perspective of the issue of finances to peel the wisdom from these pages and experience the fruitful life and prosperity that results from applying these time-tested precepts of God." **Dr. Myles Munroe, Best-Selling Author and Speaker**

"Wow!!! **Stop Robbing Peter to Pay Paul** is a hidden gem. The way in which Vicky blends the Scriptures with real life principles and practices is masterful. I found myself highlighting about 80% of the book; the information was so profound and fruitful. Vicky, you nailed it!" **Ken Brown, Award-winning author of A Leap of Faith, McDonalds Franchise Owner & Success Coach**

"Min. Vicky Love is a woman of principles and grace. She is a dynamic writer, author, teacher and preacher. She also has great wisdom and knowledge as it relates to finances. She is a kingdom builder who uses kingdom principles to motivate us to walk in victory in every area of our lives." **Chiffon F. Myricks, Conference Host and Author of A New Heart and a New Spirit, Overland Park, Kansas**

"**Stop Robbing Peter to Pay Paul** deals with practical spiritual principles on finance. In order to deal with any problem effectively, you have to cut the root. That is exactly what this book does! The first few chapters explain the root of the problem and the rest help you to re-root and start growing into a spiritually prosperous person. I love the book and the principles, it has changed my life!" **Betina M. Small, Senior Paralegal**

"I'm reading your book, **Stop Robbing Peter to Pay Paul**. It is fantastic! It's just what the Lord ordered for me at this moment in my life. I think you've done a phenomenal job. It's fabulous, it's dynamic, it's accurate, it's truthful, yet it's kind. To be honest with you, I could not put your book down. I read it from the acknowledgements all the way up to page 60 without putting it down!" **Johnny Hawkins, Attorney**

"AWESOME, SPIRIT FILLED BOOK!! I finished reading the book a week ago!! I have been so busy telling everyone to order it that I forgot to tell you how phenomenal your book is. **Stop Robbing Peter to Pay Paul** is a Bible-based guide on being a better steward of God's money. It's an easy read! I am going to recommend it to everyone I know!! Thank you for such a great work! **Yvette St.Clair, Smyrna, Georgia**

"God bless you for opening our mind to know how God wants us to be in financial blessing that we can be able to promote the gospel of Jesus Christ and save lives. Thank you for **Stop Robbing Peter to Pay Paul."** **Kossi Leo Dougba-Maglo, Wiesbaden, Germany**

"This book is great! I tell everybody about it. Generations of debt were broken in my life by the words of this book." **Norman Shuford, Real Estate Investor**

Pat Stokes,
Walk in Gods
prosperity
Vicky Spring Love

$top
robbing
Peter
to pay Paul

Dr. Vicky Spring Love

Victory Jubilee Publishing
Southfield, Michigan 48037

Unless otherwise indicated, all Scripture quotations are from the Holy Bible, King James Version. Scripture quotations marked NIV are from the Holy Bible, New International Version, © 1973, 1978, 1984 by the International Bible Society. All rights reserved. All additions with italics or underline are the author's addition.

Please note that the name, satan, and related names are not capitalized. The author chooses not to acknowledge him, even to the point of violating grammatical rules.

Every effort has been made to present accurate information in this book. However, this book is not a substitute for professional financial or legal advice.

STOP ROBBING PETER TO PAY PAUL

Vicky Spring Love
Victory Jubilee Publishing
P. O. Box 3286
Southfield, Michigan 48037

Web site: www.StopRobbingPeter.com
E-mail: vickyspringlove@hotmail.com

ISBN: 978-0-9746883-2-9
Printed in the United States of America

Cover Design by: Larry T. Jordan, Pure Praise Graphics

DEDICATION

This book is dedicated

to the memory of my mother,

Jettie Marie Spring,

a woman of dignity and discipline

who always encouraged me

to do great things for the Lord.

ACKNOWLEDGEMENTS

I thank you God for who you are and for everything you have provided in my life. You have transformed my life and taught me how to live victoriously. All that I am is because of you.

To my husband and life partner, Glen, I thank you for your continual love, support and feedback on this project. You have always believed in me and encouraged me to pursue my dreams. I am eternally grateful to you. To my children, Dante' and Tiffany, you are awesome -- continue to trust in the Lord and live out your God-given purpose.

To Pastors Larry and Sylvia Jordan of Family Victory Fellowship, your ministry has tremendously impacted my life and propelled me to walk in my divine purpose. I appreciate your practical teaching and living example of the power of God's Word. I am honored to serve in your ministry of excellence. A special thank you to Pastor Sylvia for your feedback on my manuscript and to Pastor Larry for designing my book cover – you made my book look great!

To Dr. Kenneth E. Harris, who was my pastor as a teenager, thank you for your obedience to God to teach the Word of God in season and out of season. Your in-depth knowledge of the Word and passionate Bible teaching ignited within me a love for studying the Word of God and helped me discover my ministry calling as a teacher.

To my friends and family members who have encouraged me to complete this project, I thank you for your support and prayers. You know who you are.

To all of the other pastors and ministers who have inspired me and impacted my life: Dr. Pellam Love, the late Pastor Timothy Love, Dr. Myles Munroe, Pastor Benny Hinn, and Joyce Meyer. I am forever grateful.

CONTENTS

FOREWORD

Money is a tool, a trial, and a test. If you want to expose a man's true character, give him access to large sums of money. Money reveals the heart of man and the quality of his character. The great king Solomon said, "Money answers all things." In essence, money explains everything. The poor want it. The rich hoard it. It will control those who do not control it, and destroy those who love it. Yet it is necessary for life and required for living effectively. The average man works for it, but the wise man makes it work for him. The subject of money is almost taboo, especially for the religious, yet the Bible speaks more of money than prayer and fasting.

Having the correct understanding and appreciation for this very illusive component of life is critical and must be based on biblical principles. In **Stop Robbing Peter to Pay Paul**, Vicky Spring Love presents one of the most profound, yet simple approaches to this essential subject. Her logical, yet deeply spiritual presentation of these biblical principles for financial management, giving and receiving, provide a balanced view of a much-misunderstood topic.

I encourage anyone who wants to have a fundamental perspective of the issue of finances to peel the wisdom from these pages and experience the fruitful life and prosperity that result from applying these time-tested precepts of God.

Dr. Myles Munroe
President
Bahamas Faith Ministries International
Nassau, Bahamas

9

STOP ROBBING PETER TO PAY PAUL

Introduction

We live in a society where we have been programmed for instant gratification. When we go to a fast food restaurant, we expect immediate service. If we have to wait in line, and it takes more than five minutes, we ask, "What's going on? Why are they so slow?" When we cook rice, we don't want the slow-cooking kind, we want it to be ready in an instant!

When we buy a new home, we want it completely redecorated and fully furnished within 30 days. In prior generations, our parents would buy a new home and then spend the next 20-30 years furnishing it exactly the way they wanted. But then, a lot of them suffered through the depression, which gave them a completely different mindset towards money. For most of them, debt was simply not an option.

Technology has literally transformed the way we do many things. We often cook and reheat our meals using a microwave because it's faster than a stove. In prior generations, many people washed clothes by hand and hung them up outside to dry. Now practically everyone uses an automatic washer and dryer to do those tasks. Technological advances have been designed to help us do more and more things at a faster and faster pace. At times we are moving so fast that we find it difficult to find satisfaction.

We want everything instantly. We don't want to have to wait for anything. Why is that? I believe we have been programmed by society for instant gratification. The commercials on television and radio, for instance, all suggest that we should get what we want right now, and many of those ads even offer to finance our desires!

STOP ROBBING PETER TO PAY PAUL

Television shows program us to believe that problems can be solved in 30 minutes or less. Think about it, in a 30-minute television program, they present to you a problem, show all the different angles of that problem, develop the personalities of the characters involved in the problem and then solve it. Then, we become programmed by television that our problems should be solved quickly as well.

Instant gratification programming permeates our desires for material things and becomes an insidious trap for our finances. The proliferation of credit cards makes getting things "instantly" even easier. The result is millions of people who are drowning in debt struggling to rob Peter in order to pay Paul. The result also is an astronomical increase in personal bankruptcies, which wreck devastation not only on a person's finances but many times on their family relationships as well. Money problems have been cited as a major problem in the break up of marriages.

In my household, at least twice a week, sometimes five times a week, I get a letter in the mail saying, "You have been pre-approved for this credit card..." If you haven't made a decision about your finances before that letter comes in the mail, you can get entrapped in this world's credit card mess. Because I have made decisions regarding my finances, I know where to put these credit offers -- in file 13, the garbage! I want my finances to give glory to God. God has said that we are more than conquerors through Christ Jesus and I believe that we can have victory in the area of our finances as well.

Over the past several years, I have had the opportunity to view thousands of people's finances under a microscope as they were attempting to qualify for a mortgage loan to buy or refinance a home. In recent years, over 50 percent of my business (unfortunately) has come from debt consolidation refinances. In a debt consolidation refinance, the people have credit cards that are out of control and the only way that they can get a fresh start is to take cash out of their home via a mortgage so that they can consolidate their bills. I always counsel the people to cut up their credit cards and begin operating on a cash budget. I also counsel them to make extra payments on their mortgage if they can in order to cut their interest expense.

In my business, I have dealt with clients from every economic level: low, moderate, and high income. The one common denominator that I've noticed that transcends all socio-economic barriers is this: most people spend more than they earn.

I met with a young woman attempting to purchase her first home, a small, modest home, nothing fancy. Her income was low, yet she had about $4,000 in credit card debts and a car loan. Because of her debts, she couldn't qualify to buy a home. She had too much debt for her income level.

I've met with hundreds of middle-income families who routinely carry $10-15,000 of credit card debt. But I was completely astonished when I met with a medical doctor who earned $385,000 a year and was carrying a whopping $80,000 in credit card and personal debt! In addition, he had student loans, car loans and mortgage debt. I immediately counseled him and his wife to use the prosperity that God had blessed them with to begin operating on cash and thankfully they took my advice.

After viewing the financial situations of so many debt-ridden people, I began to ask myself some questions. When is enough enough? When do you make enough money to start going through life on cash? When do you stop robbing Peter to pay Paul and start living within your means? When do you begin to enjoy the blessings of prosperity and walk away from the curses of debt? I came to the conclusion that it is not a matter of how much money you earn, but it is a matter of looking at your internal motivations for why you spend money and knowing how to manage that money. How much money you make is not as important as what you do with what you have! This is true for every economic level of society.

This brings us to the purpose of this book. This book is for you if you are behind the financial eight ball caught between maintaining a certain lifestyle on one hand and dodging creditors on the other. This book is for you if you want to get out of debt but can't seem to ever pay off those bills. This book is for you if you are simply tired of the anxiety and frustration that managing your money causes. Stop Robbing Peter to Pay Paul will help you find true financial freedom and peace of mind. This book will put you on the path towards financial victory. It will lead you step-by-step through a process of deliverance, change, strategies and results.

This book is divided into three sections – Attitude, Budget and Contentment, or as I call it – the ABC's of Financial Victory. Before we can even discuss financial strategies, we need to have a total paradigm shift in attitude. Too many people have defined their attitudes about money from the world's perspective. We need to ask ourselves what motivates us to spend more money than we make. We often try to satisfy unmet needs in our lives through our finances. But understanding our internal motivations is only the starting point. After we understand why we do what we do and gain deliverance from those things, we need to learn Godly principles that we can use to give us a new attitude towards money. But we will still have the consequences of our actions to deal with -- our messed up finances.

This leads me to the second section, Budget. "Budget" is not a four-letter word! Many people have been overwhelmed and frustrated by trying to live on a budget but I will give you practical strategies for making a budget work painlessly. A budget is simply a plan of action for the use of your finances. A wise person plans ahead. I will share with you a concrete plan of action for getting out of debt and getting back on the right track. Next I will introduce you to sound investment ideas that you can implement to reach true financial freedom.

The final section, Contentment, really comes as a result of following the strategies under Attitude and Budget. A Godly attitude towards your finances, plus a sound budget will lead to contentment in the area of your finances. On the other hand, if you choose to keep the world's attitude towards your finances and never implement a budget, it will only lead to chaos in your finances, as you probably have already experienced.

I believe and have experienced that we can live a life of victory in our finances -- day in and day out. I will share with you what God has taught me in this area. My prayer for you is that you will fully submit to God's will for your finances. And as you do, you will discover the peace and joy of financial victory! It's time for us to start our journey towards financial victory. Get ready because your finances and your life are about to be changed forever.

Vicky Spring Love

STOP ROBBING PETER TO PAY PAUL

SECTION ONE

ATTITUDE

Do not conform any longer to the pattern of this world, but be transformed by the renewing of your mind. Then you will be able to test and approve what God's will is – his good, pleasing and perfect will.

Romans 12:2 (NIV)

1

YOUR MINDSET MOTIVATES
YOUR SPENDING

It may surprise you but most money problems are not money problems at all. Many people have gone to seminars on money management or read books on budgeting only to find that their situation did not change. That is because the problem was not money. The Bible says in Matthew 6:21, "For where your treasure is, there will your heart be also." This passage of Scripture lets us know that when we look at a person's treasure, or finances, it gives us an indication of where their heart is. In other words, your financial situation is a reflection of the deeper matters of your heart, whether good or bad. If I really want to know where your heart is, I just need to look at your checkbook, your charge card statements, or your credit report.

Your use of money reflects your relationship with God and your family, your feelings of self-worth, your level of peace of mind, your feelings regarding other people, your ability to forgive, your level of discipline and your sense of purpose in life. If there are areas of emotional hurt and pain in your life that have not been resolved, it will surface in the use of your finances. If you are walking in unforgiveness with your spouse or other family members, it will surface in your spending habits. If you feel unworthy, the things you purchase will reflect that.

God is interested in our total victory from the inside out. That is why we must deal with the motivations that cause us to overspend money. God has given me tremendous insight into the motivations of people I have observed. I have noticed several reasons why people tend to misuse their finances. Perhaps you may find yourself in some of these examples.

Low Self-Esteem

A person who does not believe in their innate value will overspend money buying clothes and material things to make up for their low self-esteem. Frequently people who grow up in environments where they received conditional love become compulsive in some area of their lives as adults. Conditional love says, 'I'll love you if you do this' or 'I'll love you when you behave properly.' Whenever you misbehaved as a child, you not only felt punished, you felt *unloved*. People who were abused as a child also grow up feeling worthless because the atrocities of their past stripped them of their sense of value. Because this basic need for self-esteem is missing in your life, you are searching for it. Only you're using a credit card to try and find it.

A friend of mine, Stephanie (not her real name), used to always come to church dressed in designer clothes every Sunday. Everything matched from head to toe and it was all very expensive. In fact, she would frequently take weekend shopping trips to New York City just to go shopping. We were in our early twenties at the time and none of us had jobs that allowed for that type of extravagant wardrobe. I knew Stephanie's situation. She worked in a job where her income was inconsistent. Yet she continued to spend money on clothes that she really could not afford.

After the bills began to mount up, the pressure became too much to bear. Stephanie admitted in a fellowship gathering that she was turning over her compulsive shopping problem to the Lord for Him to deliver her. God began to show her that she was really using her overspending to make up on the outside for what was lacking on the inside. On the inside, Stephanie felt dirty and unloved because she had been sexually molested as a teenager. How beautiful it was to see God heal her and bathe her in His unconditional love. Once she accepted God's love and allowed Him to heal her damaged emotions, she no longer felt the need to overspend on extravagant clothing.

Allow God to heal your low self-esteem. He can give you a proper self-image based upon His Word. The Bible says in Psalms 139:14, " I will praise thee; for I am fearfully and wonderfully made. Marvelous are thy works, and that my soul knoweth right well." The beautiful thing about you is that God made you an original. You can search the entire earth and you will never find another human being with your same fingerprints. God made you wonderful and marvelous. God also made you to be like Him, according Genesis 1:27, "So God created man in his own image, in the image of God created he him; male and female, created he them."

Study the Scriptures for the verses that tell you how special you are to God and allow the power of God's Word to give you a new image. Renew your mind with God's Word and begin to fight satan with Scriptures as he attempts to put thoughts of low self-worth in your mind. (Romans 12:1-2; Matthew 4:1-11).

If you were abused in the past, you need the Holy Spirit to deliver you. You may have never connected the abuse of your past with the financial mess of your present, but the connection is there. One of the tactics that satan uses to keep you bound is your silence. Frequently, a person who was physically or sexually abused as a child will hide that painful memory in the deep recesses of their mind. If that person is you, please know that the first step towards your deliverance is confession. James 5:16 says,

"Confess your faults one to another and pray one for another, that ye may be healed. The effectual, fervent prayer of a righteous man availeth much." You need to find a spiritually mature Christian that you can share that painful experience with so they can pray for your deliverance and emotional healing. Recognize that your total emotional healing will take time. But as you allow the Holy Spirit to guide you, He will transform your mind and emotions by the power of His Word and His presence.

Keeping Up With the Joneses

Unfortunately, our society does an exceptional job of promoting this value to the masses. We are encouraged repeatedly through flashy advertisements and suggestive slogans that we must have a certain item simply because it is what everyone else has. Keeping up with the Joneses comes from that old myth, "the grass is greener on the other side." We look at someone else's grass and conclude that their grass is somehow better than ours so we want it. We forget that their grass has weeds in it just like ours!

When we become motivated by the desire to keep up with the Joneses, we overspend money trying to impress people that we have the "right" stuff. When we fall prey to this myth, it really stems from a lack of individual purpose. In creating you, God designed you for a specific purpose and calling. In Jeremiah 1:5, God told the prophet Jeremiah, "Before I formed thee in the belly, I knew thee; and before thou camest forth out of the womb, I sanctified thee, and ordained thee a prophet unto the nations."

God called and anointed Jeremiah before he was even in his mother's womb. Likewise, God establishes our purpose in the earth first, then He selects which mother and father will be best suited to bring us forth into the earth. God has placed you on this earth for a specific purpose that only you can fulfill. Your assignment is to discover that purpose, develop your gifts and talents and then use them with the help of Holy Spirit to fulfill your God-ordained purpose. Once you make a decision to live a life of purpose and destiny, that decision begins to affect the use of your finances as well. You will become less concerned with the Joneses. In fact you will become so focused towards accomplishing your purpose that you will have little time left for trying to impress others.

Another reason why people try to keep up with the Joneses is because of an inordinate desire for the approval of others. Perhaps you have dealt with more than your share of rejection in your life and so to compensate for it, you have become a people pleaser. In buying all the latest trends, you are trying to win the approval of people, and prove that you really are acceptable.

The problem with this motivation for spending is that no matter what you do, there will always be people who will not approve of you. If the religious leaders rejected Jesus, the Son of God, we should not be surprised when people reject us as well. We need to get our approval from God and be satisfied with it. Galatians 1:10 in the NIV says, "Am I now trying to win the approval of men, or of God? Or am I trying to please men? If I were still trying to please men, I would not be a servant of Christ."

This verse delivered me from the need for other people's approval. This verse says that if I'm trying to please men, then I am not Christ's servant. That is a heavy statement. With all my heart, I want to be Christ's servant, so I cannot allow the approval or disapproval of people to influence me. The answer is to focus on what God says and to allow His peace to rule in my heart.

Status Conscious

People who are status conscious are people who feel that they have "arrived." By the world's standards, they have achieved a high level of success. Perhaps they have advanced college degrees, or they have reached a high position in a corporation or in their own business. So they feel compelled to surround themselves with all the material things that confirm their level of success to the rest of the world. The problem is that most people overspend no matter what economic level they are on. We have all heard the stories of entertainers who have 25 custom cars, 200 fur coats and huge entourages of people on their payrolls. When they later fall out of the limelight, they wonder where all their money went.

A person who is status conscious can also be a person who does not have a lot of real wealth in terms of a high income or money in the bank. However, they may be using credit cards to finance the illusion that they are more successful than they really are.

Don't misunderstand me; there is nothing wrong with buying nice clothes and material things that you can afford. But God is always looking at your heart. What is your motivation for buying things? Do you own things or do the things own you? In other words, if you lost all your "stuff" tomorrow, would you still have the peace of God in your heart? Remember what God says in Luke 12:15, "And he said unto them, Take heed, and beware of covetousness: for a man's life consisteth not in the abundance of the things which he possesseth." You should not define yourself by what you own but instead by whom you belong to!

If you are status conscious, it affects your relationships with people. You may find yourself talking down to people or expecting everyone to cater to your desires. This is particularly dangerous because it is based upon a spirit of pride. Our God is love, mercy, kindness, forgiveness and much more. But one of the six things that the Lord hates is pride according to Proverbs 6:16-19. If you desire the Lord's blessing upon your finances, your mindset cannot be based on a spirit of pride. The Word of God gives a strong prophetic word on pride in Proverbs 16:18, "Pride goeth before destruction, and an haughty spirit before a fall." If you don't want destruction to come into your life, then renounce that spirit of pride now in the name of Jesus and begin to live according to God's way of doing things.

God's way is for us to put other people's needs before our own. He tells us in Philippians 2:3, "Let nothing be done through strife or vainglory; but in lowliness of mind let each esteem others better than themselves." God never gives anyone a license to look down on others, for He says in Romans 12:3, "For I say, through the grace given unto me, to every man that is among you, not to think of himself more highly than he ought to think; but to think soberly, according as God hath dealt to every man the measure of faith." God considers each person important to Him.

If God has blessed you to achieve high levels of success or wealth, you need to realize that He has established a purpose for your wealth. You were not given wealth to simply increase the amount of toys that you own, but rather to establish His kingdom and minister to the needs of others. Deuteronomy 8:18 says, "But thou shalt remember the LORD thy God: for it is he that giveth thee power to get wealth, that he may establish his covenant which he sware unto thy fathers, as it is this day."

Knowing that God alone allows us to obtain wealth should keep us humble. We should never forget that we are sent here as ambassadors of the kingdom of God. Our job description is to use whatever resources we have been blessed with in order to bless others and lead them to Christ.

Control Tactics in Marriage

Married couples sometimes use money as a method of control. After an argument, the wife decides to go shopping at the mall to get back at her husband. The husband is mad at the wife so he decides to go play golf more than the budget allows. This basically amounts to using money for revenge. This can prove to be a very destructive game to play. When we try to manipulate our spouses into doing what we want, what we are really trying to do is play God in that person's life. We don't have patience for people to grow in the fear and admonition of the Lord, we selfishly want them to change now, so we play games with each other.

A friend of mine, who I'll call Cynthia, had an argument with her husband over whether or not it was a good time to purchase a new car. Instead of discussing the matter further and trying to reach a compromise, she decided to go ahead and buy the car without his consent. She figured that since she worked and was bringing money into the house, she could buy whatever she wanted. So she just drove home one day with the new car. Needless to say, that car became the source of many arguments and grief in their marriage. She regretted that she had ever made that decision. It planted a seed of distrust and vengeance in their relationship. You want to be careful what seeds you plant, because sooner or later, they will produce a harvest!

We use money as a method of control because we don't want to follow God's plan for relationships. God has clearly outlined His plan for marriage relationships in Ephesians 5:18-33. Take time to read this passage of Scripture. I believe the key to successful marriages starts with each individual having a right relationship with God, being filled with the Spirit and having their thoughts and lifestyle in line with God's Word. When you begin to focus your time and attention on improving yourself, you have little time to control your spouse. We are also told to be thankful to God for all things, even the difficult times. When you have a thankful heart, God can begin to wrap His loving purpose around your situation to bring the peace of mind that you desire.

I remember a time when my husband and I were going through a real distressful season in our marriage and I was crying out to God for help. I would lament to God about all the things that I felt my husband was doing wrong and plead for God to change him. I'll never forget one time when I was crying out to God and God spoke to me quite clearly. The words He spoke to me slapped me in the face and knocked me to my knees. He said, "When you stand before me at the judgment seat of Christ, I am not going to ask you what kind of husband Glen has been, I am going to ask you what kind of wife you have been." God really got my attention. He caused me to refocus my attention from my husband to myself. The only person you can ever control is yourself.

The second key to a successful marriage is that the husband and wife need to submit to one another. This is critically important for the success of any relationship. God did not give all the gifts and talents to the husband as the head of the home and leave the wife as a mindless slave at his beck and call. All throughout the Bible, God used women in key roles to affect all of mankind. And He is still using women today. Usually, God will bring a certain man and woman together as husband and wife because they have complementary gifts and talents. In other words, the areas that I am weak in are the areas that my husband is strong in and vice versa.

To give you an example, when my husband and I first got married, I naively thought that since he was the man he should handle the finances. So I would give him my paycheck and let him pay the bills. After only two months, my husband came to me totally frustrated because he just didn't like handling the finances. He asked if I wanted to do it. I leaped at the opportunity because all my life I have enjoyed managing money and have always been good at it. As a child, my siblings nicknamed me "the banker". So I began handling the finances in our home, which means that I am responsible for setting up the budget, depositing all checks, paying all bills, and making sure that we are saving for future goals like the children's college education and retirement. My husband submits to me in the handling of the finances because I am the one who is most skillful at it. However, just because I manage the finances does not mean that I make all the decisions. We discuss all major purchases and make those decisions jointly.

The third key to a successful marriage is that wives are to submit to their husbands as unto the Lord. God has set order in the home, with the man being the head. The role of the wife is not a subordinate role but a different role. Notice that God commanded the wife to submit to the husband, he never told the husband to *make* his wife submit through intimidation or control as some men try to do. It has to be the wife's decision to submit out of obedience to the Lord. In submitting to the husband, the wife is showing him reverence and respect. My husband is my covering and my protection.

The fourth key to a successful marriage is for the husband to love his wife as Christ loved the church and as he loves his own body. Christ loved the church sacrificially with such a depth of love that He laid down His life for the church. A husband should have such a great love for his wife that he is willing to make sacrifices for her. A man should love his wife like he loves himself. This implies that if a man does not have a proper love for himself, he will have difficulty showing love for his wife.

Allow God to be God. Give your spouse back to God and pray for him or her. Don't try to use your finances to control your spouse or manipulate them into doing what you want. As we begin to refocus our attention from our spouses to ourselves, we begin to see our own shortcomings that we need to work on. You become free to develop your potential and be all that God has called and ordained you to be. But more importantly, you begin to lovingly accept the shortcomings in your spouse and allow him or her space to grow in God's timing and purpose for their life.

Anxiety

Some people are so worried about tomorrow that they cannot enjoy today. According to Webster's dictionary, to be anxious means to be worried or uneasy about what may happen. Anxiety is a form a fear. I read a story once of a couple who had over $1 million in the bank. However, because they had grown up in poor homes, they refused to spend this money to even provide basis necessities for their children. Their children wore second-hand clothes. They shopped for groceries at a place that sold canned goods that had passed their expiration date. This was very extreme. But because they had never been delivered from the pain of growing up in poverty, they could not enjoy even the basic comforts of life much less the prosperity that was available to them. They were afraid they would run out of money so they never spent any of it. Their fear of poverty caused them to live in poverty even though they had $1 million at their disposal.

Growing up in a home where money is tight can affect your view of money today. If you're not careful, you will reenact the poverty of your past. Or you will go to the other extreme and overindulge yourself to compensate for what you feel you missed as a child. This is also based on fear. You are not sure you will have enough so you stockpile things in order to feel secure.

I am reminded of the parable of the rich man who reaped a great harvest (Luke 12:16-21). But instead of sharing his crops with others, he decided to tear down his barns and build bigger barns to store his grain in. Then he would be able to relax and take it easy for the rest of his life. Unfortunately for him, that was the last day of his life. So someone else got to enjoy his great harvest.

God gives us a solution to our feelings of anxiety. It is based on our faith in God. When we have faith in God as the source of our supply, we will not fall prey to either the extreme of not spending any money or the extreme of overindulging ourselves. In Philippians 4:6-7, we are given a formula to cure our anxiety. We are told to not be anxious for anything, but to pray about everything with thanksgiving. When we pray, we acknowledge God as our supply. We depend completely on Him. He alone meets all of our needs. As we rest in knowing His supply is unlimited, we can be delivered from the need to over spend or under spend. Our fear is replaced with faith, and we can walk in His peace of mind.

Undisciplined

If you have not found yourself in any of the other examples, perhaps you are just undisciplined and uninformed in the use of your finances. Throughout our educational system, we have failed miserably to teach people how to handle a household budget. Our colleges and universities teach people knowledge and skills to get a well-paying job, but rarely do they offer a class titled, "Household Budgeting 101". So we are left to ourselves to determine how to spend our earnings. Unfortunately, we usually get enticed by the advertisements of the world and end up over-extended and in debt.

YOUR MINDSET MOTIVATES YOUR SPENDING

If you are like most people, you do not have a written budget, so you live from paycheck to paycheck, spending every dollar as soon as you receive it and wondering where it all went at the end of the month. Sadly, you are probably two weeks away from personal bankruptcy. In other words, if you got a notice that you will be laid off in two weeks, you would have no way of paying your bills after you got your last paycheck.

Our God is a God of order and discipline. He wants you to add up the costs before you start building the house. He wants you to be disciplined in handling money.

2

ARE YOU AN OWNER OR A MANAGER?

When you look at your financial situation, how do you view yourself? Do you see yourself as managing your own money or do you see yourself as managing someone else's money? If you are honest, most people will say they see themselves as managing their own money because that is what this society has conditioned us to believe. However, we are not of this world and so our mindset again needs to be transformed by Biblical standards.

We have been taught by the world that we are owners. "I pulled myself up by my own bootstraps." "I did it my way." "I am a self-made man." These are just a few of the ideologies that have impacted our thinking. As an owner, we believe that we are the owner of our talents, skills, knowledge and abilities. We go to school to develop these attributes and determine which career to pursue. Once we start earning a living, the money we make is ours to decide how to spend.

Learn From the Israelites

In the book of Haggai, the people of God had gotten caught up in taking care of their own business. They had built up their own houses, were working hard in their business of agriculture, were earning wages and trying to progress in life. However, there was a problem. In their quest for success, they neglected the house of God. And God was not pleased. When our efforts do not include God, they do not qualify for the blessings of God. God is a

33

jealous God; He wants to be Lord of our lives. The Lord challenged the people through the prophet Haggai.

Haggai 1:3-11

[3]Then came the word of the LORD by Haggai the prophet, saying, [4]Is it time for you, O ye, to dwell in your cieled houses, and this house lie waste? [5]Now therefore thus saith the LORD of hosts; consider your ways. [6]Ye have sown much, and bring in little; ye eat, but ye have not enough; ye drink, but ye are not filled with drink; ye clothe you, but there is none warm; and he that earneth wages earneth wages to put it into a bag with holes. [7]Thus saith the LORD of hosts; consider your ways. [8]Go up to the mountain, and bring wood, and build the house; and I will take pleasure in it, and I will be glorified, saith the LORD. [9]Ye looked for much, and, lo, it came to little; and when ye brought it home, I did blow upon it. Why? saith the LORD of hosts. Because of mine house that is waste, and ye run every man unto his own house. [10]Therefore the heaven over you is stayed from dew, and the earth is stayed from her fruit. [11]And I called for a drought upon the land, and upon the mountains, and upon the corn, and upon the new wine, and upon the oil, and upon that which the ground bringeth forth, and upon men, and upon cattle, and upon all the labour of the hands.

God was angry with the people because they had forgotten Him as Lord. Initially after coming out of Babylonian captivity, the Israelites were excited about rebuilding the temple to worship God. They set up an altar, appointed the Levites as priests and assigned workers to complete the temple. The foundation was laid with excitement and exuberance. After the foundation was laid, the Israelites encountered opposition from the political leaders and were ordered by a governmental decree to stop building the temple. The Israelites yielded to this opposition.

Years went pass, the political forces that opposed them were long gone, the governmental decree was reversed; yet the Israelites still neglected the temple. They had lost their purpose, their passion and their sense of urgency to build God's house. Instead, they were focused on working their jobs, building a nice home for themselves and enjoying their lifestyle. (Read Ezra 3:8-4:24 for background.) Like many of us, they had allowed the "cares of this world" to cause them to procrastinate on the more important things of God.

Consider Your Ways

Notice carefully what God says through the prophet Haggai in chapter 1, verses 5 and 6, "Consider your ways." In other words, evaluate the results your efforts are producing. Although on the surface it may appear that you are making progress, you are really just treading water.

Likewise, you may have gotten promotions on your job, pay increases, bigger houses and fancier cars. However, are you still living from paycheck to paycheck? At the end of the month, do you still wonder where your money went? Do you work really hard, yet you never seem to be able to pay off your debts, much less save anything for the future? Consider your ways. Are you putting your money in a bag with holes in it?

The Israelites never achieved their potential while they were neglecting God's house. They may have reasoned to themselves that they didn't have the time, energy or resources to build God's house. The thing they failed to realize though is that because they did not reverence God's house, He withdrew His blessings from their efforts. When you make a sacrifice for God's house, He will multiply and bless the time you have left to pursue your business efforts. He will help you to redeem your time or maximize the use of your time.

God allowed the elements of nature to work against the efforts of the Israelites. God is sovereign, He controls the elements, and therefore, He can position things to be in your favor or position things to be against you. I don't know about you but I would never want to be in a position where God is against me.

The Israelites had allowed their devotion to God to be diluted by their daily lifestyle. In essence, they had become lords of their own lives. They felt they could produce crops, enjoy their families, build their own homes and then fit God into their lifestyle when it was convenient. They were in charge of their own finances and provisions. But God never called us to be owners; He has charged us with the responsibility of managing His assets and being accountable to Him for our actions.

We are Managers of God's Assets

Think of it like an owner of business. If I own a shoe store, for example, then I am in charge of all of operations of that facility. I put marketing plans in place to generate revenues and control expenses so that I can earn a profit. I can decide that out of the profits of my business I am going to give a gift to John. Would John have the right to ask to look at my financial records to see if I could have given him a larger gift? Of course not, he should just be grateful for the gift.

Let's change this scenario a little. Now I am manager of a shoe store that John owns. He has delegated responsibility for day-to-day operations of the store to me. He has instructed me on the marketing plans to use to generate revenues and the expenses to control so that I generate a profit. Now I write a check to John. Does John have the right to ask to see the complete financial records of the business? Of course he does, he is the owner of the company and I work for him.

God tells us in His Word that we are managers of His assets. We can go all the way back to Genesis to establish this fact. God created the heavens and the earth. Whenever someone creates something, they own it. In our society, people obtain patents, copyrights, or trademarks in order to protect the ownership of something that they have created. Since God created everything, He owns it.

Psalms 50:10-12 says, "For every beast of the forest is mine, and the cattle upon a thousand hills. I know all the fowls of the mountains: and the wild beasts of the field are mine. If I were hungry, I would not tell thee: for the world is mine, and the fullness thereof."

We need to also understand that we also belong to God. We were created by God in Genesis 1:26-28, "And God said, Let us make man in our image, after our likeness: and let them have dominion over the fish of the sea, and over the fowl of the air, and over the cattle, and over all the earth, and over every creeping thing that creepeth upon the earth. So God created man in his own image, in the image of God created he him; male and female created he them. And God blessed them, and God said unto them, Be fruitful, and multiply, and replenish the earth, and subdue it: and have dominion over the fish of the sea, and over the fowl of the air, and over every living thing that moveth upon the earth."

God not only created us and owns us, but He has given us an assignment: to dominate in the earth. We are to reflect God's glory in all that we do and never forget that God is the one who has endowed us with the gifts, talents and abilities to do our work. The abilities that operate within us are because of the grace of God. "Having then gifts differing according to the grace that is given to us, whether prophecy, let us prophesy according to the proportion of faith; or ministry, let us wait on our ministering: or he that teacheth, on teaching; or he that exhorteth, on exhortation: he that giveth, let him do it with simplicity; he that ruleth, with diligence; he that sheweth mercy, with cheerfulness (Romans 12:6-8)."

The Purpose of Money

We also need to understand that God has given us a purpose for the money we earn in the earth. We are not given money to do whatever we want with it. God tells us the purpose of money in Deuteronomy 8:17-18, "And thou say in thine heart, my power and the might of mine hand hath gotten me this wealth. But thou shalt remember the LORD thy God: for it is he that giveth thee power to get wealth, that he may establish his covenant which he sware unto thy fathers, as it is this day."

The purpose of our money is to establish God's covenant in the earth. Throughout the ages, God has always sought a people who would honor Him as Lord, who would reverence Him as their source and supply, who would obey Him. In this nation we live in, the United States, we are used to a democracy, where every person has a voice in the voting process and the majority rules. But God has never been interested in a democracy, He is interested in a theocracy, which means that God is in charge and we willingly obey His statutes and commands.

There are so many people in various parts of this world who have never heard the salvation message of Jesus Christ. Evangelists and missionaries desire to go to these places. However, ministers of the gospel have to purchase airplane tickets and pay for housing just like anyone else. So it is up to the saints of God to provide the resources through our earnings to fund evangelistic efforts. God may not have spoken to you to go to the missionary field, but He has spoken to every believer through His Word to financially support the efforts of others who are called to go.

The parable of the talents in the Bible gives us many valuable lessons that we can apply to our finances.

Matthew 25:14-30

[14]For the kingdom of heaven is as a man traveling into a far country, who called his own servants, and delivered unto them his goods. [15]And unto one he gave five talents, to another two, and to another one; to every man according to his several ability; and straightway took his journey.

[16]Then he that had received the five talents went and traded with the same, and made them other five talents. [17]And likewise he that had received two, he also gained other two. [18]But he that had received one went and digged in the earth, and hid his lord's money.

[19]After a long time the lord of those servants cometh, and reckoneth with them. [20]And so he that had received five talents came and brought other five talents, saying, Lord, thou deliveredst unto me five talents: behold, I have gained beside them five talents more. [21]His lord said unto him, Well done, thou good and faithful servant: thou hast been faithful over a few things, I will make thee ruler over many things: enter thou into the joy of thy lord.

[22]He also that had received two talents came and said, Lord, thou deliveredst unto me two talents: behold, I have gained two other talents beside them. [23]His lord said unto him, Well done,

good and faithful servant; thou hast been faithful over a few things, I will make thee ruler over many things: enter thou into the joy of thy lord.

[24]Then he which had received the one talent came and said, Lord, I knew thee that thou art an hard man, reaping where thou hast not sown, and gathering where thou hast not strawed: [25]And I was afraid, and went and hid thy talent in the earth: lo, there thou hast that is thine.

[26]His lord answered and said unto him, Thou wicked and slothful servant, thou knewest that I reap where I sowed not, and gather where I have not strawed: [27]Thou oughtest therefore to have put my money to the exchangers, and then at my coming I should have received mine own with usury.

[28]Take therefore the talent from him, and give it unto him which hath ten talents. [29]For unto every one that hath shall be given, and he shall have abundance: but from him that hath not shall be taken away even that which he hath. [30]And cast ye the unprofitable servant into outer darkness: there shall be weeping and gnashing of teeth.

During biblical days, a talent was a form of currency. One talent equaled 6,000 days of wages. This Scripture has other applications but it also gives us basic guidelines on handling money. The first principle we glean from this Scripture is that God is the owner and we are managers. The Lord put each individual in charge of managing a portion of His assets.

God gave money to each individual according to his ability to handle it. Not everyone is going to be given the same amount of money to manage. One person was given five talents; another two and the last person was given one talent. However, even the person who was given only one talent was still given a lot of money to manage; he was given the equivalent of 19 years of wages lump sum at one time to manage. If you were given that much money at one time, would you know what to do with it? Some people are given more money because they are more faithful and skilled in handling it.

God Wants To Review Your Finances

Another principle we can learn from this passage is that as owner of our money, God has the right to review our use of money. What if God came to you and said, "Okay, show me your checkbook, your bank statements and your charge card statements, it's time to do an audit!" Many of us shriek at the very thought of that! But since we are only managers of God's assets, we need to constantly remind ourselves that we are accountable to Him for what we do with what He has provided for us.

This parable also teaches us that God expects multiplication of our finances and not just maintenance. The Lord was pleased with the person who was given five talents and the person who was given two talents because both were able to double His money.

God expects us to make wise financial decisions that will bless the house of God, while providing for our family today and for generations to come. Proverbs 13:22 (NIV) tells us, "A good man leaves an inheritance for his children's children, but a sinner's wealth is stored up for the righteous."

The one individual who hid the money in the earth and did not earn any interest on the money, the Lord was not pleased with him. In fact, the Lord said he was wicked and lazy.

Another principle we learn is that if you want to be promoted to the next level in your finances, you need to prove your faithfulness at your current level. The two

41

people who faithfully took care of the money that was entrusted to them were blessed and rewarded. In fact, the lazy servant's one talent was taken from him and given to the more faithful servant. When we are faithful over a few things, God will make us ruler over many things.

Many of us are looking for God to increase our incomes. Yet we can't accurately say where our current and past income has gone. We want the prosperity of God, yet we have not been faithful in what God has given us so far. If you have not been faithfully returning the tithe, giving offerings, paying your bills on time, and living within your means on your current income; then how can God trust you to faithfully handle more? Be faithful to God where you are right now and then God will promote you to another level of blessing.

Change your mindset. Begin to view your paycheck as a portion of God's assets that He is allowing you to manage. That is an awesome responsibility. With God as the owner, He has the right to inspect your financial affairs so it's time to get your house in order. Later in this book, we will discuss techniques for getting out of debt and setting up a written budget. This process will take time and effort but the rewards will be worth it. And more importantly, you will be honoring God by managing His money in a more productive manner.

3

Beware of satan's Devices

Satan is a liar and a deceiver. When he comes to you with an idea, it's important to remember that he will never come to you dressed in a red suit with a pitchfork and a megaphone making a loud announcement, "Do what I say and I guarantee it will destroy your life!" He is not going to do that. Instead he will come to you with a suggestion that seems like a good idea. He may even misquote a Scripture to substantiate what he is saying. But beware, his only joy is in destroying people's lives.

When he came to Eve in the Garden of Eden in Genesis Chapter 3, he started out by saying, "hath God said, Ye shall not eat of every tree of the garden?" The woman's first mistake was to enter into a dialogue with satan. That was a mistake because satan is a master manipulator, filled with cunning strategies designed to deceive and destroy. Satan then begins to convince the woman that God didn't really mean that they would die if they ate of the fruit. He told her that she would be like God, knowing good and evil. So he starts out by misquoting God, and he does the same thing today.

If Eve had really thought about it, she would have realized that she was already made in the image of God, according to Genesis 1:26, "And God said, Let us make man in our image, after our likeness: and let them have dominion over the fish of the sea, and over the fowl of the air, and over the cattle, and over all the earth, and over every creeping thing that creepeth upon the earth."

Being made in God's image meant that like God, man and woman were spiritual beings who possess a mind, a will and emotions. Because there was no sin in this state of innocence, Adam and Eve had an absolutely perfect existence. They lived in the presence of God 24 hours a day. There was no sickness or disease, no heartache or pain, no lack, just the fullness of joy that comes from being in God's presence. What more could a person want?

Satan, through his cunning, deceptive strategies, was able to get the woman to doubt what God had said; he was able to get her focus off of obedience and onto fulfilling her own personal desires. Satan deceived her into thinking she was lacking something when she in fact lived in a perfect existence. He made her think she could have something more exciting if she would just follow his plan.

Adam's problem in the garden was that he refused to exercise the authority that God had given to him. When God created man and woman, He had given them dominion over the earth and all the animals. To have dominion means to dominate, to control, to rule over, and to master. Satan used the body of the serpent to speak to Eve. However, Adam was right there with her. He should have used his dominion authority to rebuke the serpent and tell it to be quiet, but he didn't.

The result was sin in Genesis 3:6, "And when the woman saw that the tree was good for food, and that it was pleasant to the eyes, and a tree to be desired to make one wise, she took of the fruit thereof, and did eat, and gave also unto her husband with her; and he did eat."

When sin occurred, it brought spiritual death and separation from the presence of God. Satan had promised an exciting adventure but it turned out to be a horrible nightmare. Satan is just as subtle and deceptive today. All of his plans and strategies for destruction are wrapped up in exciting, fun-filled, enticing, seemingly harmless ideas.

We will explore some of his tactics and expose them for the destruction they bring in people's lives.

The Love of Money

One of the key strategies of satan is to get people entrapped with the love of money. When you love money, it becomes your god, your obsession, what you constantly focus on. The love of money is not just a malady of the rich, even poor people can have a love of money. It depends what your constant focus is. God never intended for us to focus all of energy on how much money we have or don't have. An offshoot of the love of money is an inordinate desire for possessions – big houses, fancy cars, more clothes than you can wear – status symbols of success.

The Word of God lets us know that there are two masters in this world. They are not God and satan; they are God and money. These two masters are competing for your devotion; you have to decide which one you will serve. "No man can serve two masters: for either he will hate the one, and love the other; or else he will hold to the one, and despise the other. Ye cannot serve God and mammon (Matthew 6:24)."

God intends for us to use money as a tool to establish His kingdom in the earth and to bless people's lives. But He never intended for us to become obsessed with how much money we have. The Bible says, "For the love of money is the root of all evil: which while some coveted after, they have erred from the faith, and pierced themselves through with many sorrows (1 Timothy 6:10)."

It's important to note that money is neither good nor evil; it is the love of money that is wrong. When you become obsessed with making money, it can cause you to compromise your morals and principles in order to obtain it. You decide to skip church and give up serving in ministry in order to work more than what is required.

Money has to always be regarded as a tool. As a tool, it can be used for good or bad – it takes on the morals of the person who owns it. One million dollars in the hands of a God-fearing evangelist will be used to reach more souls for the kingdom. However, the same money in the hands of a drug lord will be used to bring more drugs to the streets. When money becomes your master, it can destroy your life. But when money is your servant, it can bless your life and the lives of others.

Deceitfulness

We know that satan is a liar as Jesus proclaimed to the Pharisees, "Ye are of your father the devil, and the lusts of your father ye will do. He was a murderer from the beginning, and abode not in the truth, because there is no truth in him. When he speaketh a lie, he speaketh of his own: for he is a liar, and the father of it (John 8:44)." Since satan is a deceiver, it is no wonder that he would motivate people to engage in deceitful practices as a method of getting ahead in life. To deceive means to lie, to cheat, and to be dishonest. Some things you may consider harmless acts, but remember we serve a holy God who cannot bless deceptive acts.

I know someone, I'll call him Jason, who when he goes to the movies will routinely pay for one movie and then when it is over, sneak into another movie to watch it without paying for it. He thinks he's getting the second movie for free. No one sees him so he thinks he's gotten away with it. The reality though it that he has just stolen that second movie, he is a thief. No he didn't go into a store and shove a watch in his pocket and then leave without paying for it, but he did steal nonetheless.

The spirit of deception is a spirit of stealing. Instead of trusting God to promote you in the area of your finances, you try to get ahead by little acts of deception.

I remember a time when my husband bought me a watch and a gold necklace for Christmas from the same store. The watch was not exactly what I wanted so I returned it, along with the receipt for the store clerk to give me a credit back on our charge card. The watch had cost $100; the necklace had cost $350. When the store clerk finished ringing up the return on the cash register and handed me the credit for my charge card, it was for $350. At this moment, I had a choice: I could gleam in my added "blessing" because the clerk had mistaken credited my account for $250 too much, or I could point out the mistake to the clerk. I chose to point out the mistake. The store clerk was both shocked and grateful as he said, "Thank you for pointing out that mistake to me."

Why did I point it out? Because I know that God does not bless dishonest gain. Proverbs is a book of God's wisdom that we can apply to our lives. In Proverbs 20:23 NIV, it says, "The LORD detests differing weights, and dishonest scales do not please him." This means that God is interested in us maintaining honest business dealings. Items for sale in Old Testament times were often valued by weighing them on a scale. A dishonest businessman could increase his profit on an item by using inaccurate weights to produce a false value on the scale. This was done in order to charge more for something than it was really worth. God is not pleased with that behavior.

Some people habitually lie on their tax returns that they file with the government, especially when it concerns cash income that they receive for business ventures. I cannot tell you how many people have come to me to apply for a mortgage who are self-employed and do not report their income to the government. Then they wonder why their business is not prospering or why it's more difficult for them to get approved for a mortgage. It is because God cannot bless deception. Don't get me wrong; I am in favor of taking every legitimate tax deduction available to minimize my tax liability to Uncle Sam. However, I believe in fully reporting my income and filing an honest tax return.

Even Jesus paid His taxes and encouraged His disciples to pay taxes. When the Pharisees asked Jesus if it was lawful to pay taxes, he said, "Render to Caesar the things that are Caesar's, and to God the things that are God's. And they marveled at him (Mark 12:17)." On another occasion, Jesus and Peter were approached about paying their tribute, or taxes, and Jesus readily paid His taxes.

Matthew 17:24-27

[24] And when they were come to Capernaum, they that received tribute money came to Peter, and said, Doth not your master pay tribute?

[25] He saith, Yes. And when he was come into the house, Jesus prevented him, saying, What thinkest thou, Simon? of whom do the kings of the earth take custom or tribute? of their own children, or of strangers? [26] Peter saith unto him, Of strangers.

Jesus saith unto him, Then are the children free. [27] Notwithstanding, lest we should offend them, go thou to the sea, and cast an hook, and take up the fish that first cometh up; and when thou hast opened his mouth, thou shalt find a piece of money: that take, and give unto them for me and thee.

Be honest in all of your business dealings. Know that even when you can get away with deceptive practices with man, afterwards, you may feel remorseful because God has built a conscience within you. "Bread of deceit is sweet to a man; but afterwards his mouth shall be filled with gravel (Proverbs 20:17)." You should also remind yourself that God is always watching.

We need to learn to trust God to promote us and bless us in life instead of trying to get ahead by acts of deception. Jesus has promised us an abundant life; when we seek God with our whole hearts, He will provide for all of our needs and desires.

Get Rich Quick Schemes

This world is full of get rich quick schemes designed to make you feel you can obtain riches and wealth overnight with little effort on your part. These schemes are contrary to God's plan. God's plan for prosperity is obedience, serving, giving and faithfulness. When we try to take a short cut to wealth, it only brings strife and frustration in our lives. "A faithful man will be richly blessed, but one eager to get rich will not go unpunished (Proverbs 28:20 NIV)."

One of the fastest growing schemes of the enemy is gambling. It used to be that gambling was confined to only a few major locations. Now it seems that no matter where you travel to, you can find legalized gambling. It is permeating our society. Not only are casinos being built in numerous locations, but also gambling is readily available over the Internet. There are thousands of gambling websites available on the Internet.

Of course you know that when you gamble, the odds are against your winning. The odds are always in favor of the house winning. That is why gambling brings in such huge revenues because so many people lose their money to the casino owners. But what is the lure of gambling? I believe people gamble to escape reality. You want a better life for yourself and for a brief moment while you are waiting to see if you won, you have a glimmer of hope that your life can be changed.

But that glimmer of hope quickly turns into a nightmare when you choose to gamble. Before long, you

49

begin gambling with larger and larger sums of money. Soon, the money that was supposed to be used to pay the rent or mortgage is gambled away. You may even go into debt to support your gambling habit. Yes, gambling can become an addiction. And like any other addiction, it can destroy your family and personal relationships, and cause problems on your job. Gambling is one of satan's devices – he lures you with the promise of riches, but instead he destroys your life.

I would like to challenge you if you take part in gambling activities. Instead of betting on something where the odds are against your winning, why not try a sure thing? If you have not already done so, give your life to Jesus Christ. He came to give you an abundant life. He will give your life purpose and destiny. He has promised to meet all of your needs if you will seek Him first. If you are already a believer, begin to seek God's help to solve your problems instead of looking for an easy way out through gambling.

Pyramid Schemes

A pyramid scheme is a venture where the money of new investors in a project is used to pay profit to current investors. Eventually, these schemes fall apart when you run out of new investors. Then, everyone loses money.

Some multilevel marketing companies, called MLMs for short, are actually masked pyramid schemes. MLMs are also known as network marketing companies. According to the United States Postal Inspection Service, "there are many multi-level distributorship schemes that are nothing more than sophisticated chain letters. They operate as a 'pyramid', claiming participants can earn lots of money by concentrating most, if not all, of their efforts on recruiting distributors rather than selling a product."

A lot of MLMs will recruit you with the pitch, "You're not selling, you're telling," because they know that most people are uncomfortable selling. However, the reality is that in order to sell any product or service successfully, you must be comfortable with the sales profession and be willing to develop extraordinary sales skills.

All of these companies recommend you start "telling" your friends and family about your new venture. However, if your friends and family are not interested, don't become so pushy that you offend them in the process. You shouldn't sacrifice your relationships with friends and family in your quest for success.

The lure of MLMs is that for a small fee of $15-50, you can purchase a distributor kit and be your own boss. All MLMs promise "six-figure" incomes when you reach a certain level. However, they never really outline for you the costs involved. MLM distributors end up spending hundreds to thousands of dollars buying the product or service for themselves, making phone calls, purchasing samples or sales literature, paying travel expenses to attend company seminars, etc. If you do become involved with a MLM, keep accurate financial records of your income and your expenses to determine how much profit you are really making.

There are some legitimate MLM companies. Before you get involved with any of these companies, do your homework. Check the Better Business Bureau and the state and national Attorney General's offices to see if any complaints have been filed against the company or its owners. You want to be sure it is a legitimate business with a viable product or service. Make sure that the product or service is one that you truly believe in and that you are not just trying to make money.

Laziness

God has ordained work as the method for us to obtain our financial resources. In the beginning when God created mankind, He put Adam in the Garden of Eden and gave him a job. "And the LORD God took the man, and put him into the garden of Eden to dress it and to keep it (Genesis 2:15)." Adam's job was to dress and keep the garden, in other words, to work. This assignment was given prior to the fall of man. Contrary to what some people believe, work is not part of the punishment given to man after he sinned. After the fall, work became more difficult for man, but work was part of God's divine plan from the beginning.

Some people become lazy in their work habits. They only do the minimum amount of work that is required. They come to work late, take a long lunch hour and then leave early. Then they are the first to complain when they are passed over for a promotion. Or they feel jealous when someone else launches out into their own business venture.

Then there is the group of people who always expect someone else to give them a handout. We all know someone who fits this category. It may be a family member or a friend, but whenever you see them they are asking to borrow some money. In many instances, these people don't have a job or they can't keep a job because they really don't want to put forth the disciplined effort it takes to be successful.

God has a plan for our work habits. First of all, He has given each one of us certain gifts and talents. It is our responsibility to discover our God-given gifts and talents; go to school to develop them; and then get a job or start a business that will bring in income from the use of our skills. When we follow this path, we ensure that we find the profession that will be enjoyable for us to work in.

Second, God expects us to be diligent. To be diligent means to be hardworking, disciplined and committed to whatever task you are assigned. You persevere, you are persistent, and you don't give up easily in your quest for success. You go above and beyond the basic requirements to give an excellent effort to your work.

Third, God expects you to be faithful. To be faithful means you are reliable – you are there, consistently, day-in and day-out. Your supervisor knows he or she can depend on you. When you give your word that you will complete a project by a certain time, it is like money that your employer can bank on.

The Word of God gives us a clear contrast of what happens to the diligent as opposed to the lazy person. "Diligent hands will rule, but laziness ends in slave labor (Proverbs 12:24 NIV)." This means that when you are a diligent worker you will be put in charge, you will rule. If you want to be promoted, be a faithful worker where you are now.

You should also remember that when you are working, God is really your boss and not man. Colossians 3:17 says, "And whatever ye do in word or deed, do all in the name of the Lord Jesus, giving thanks to God and the Father by him." God will bless your faithfulness to Him.

Other Devices

These are only a few of satan's deceptive devices, there are many others. Whenever you are presented with an idea for the use of your time and money, pray about it first. God desires to direct His children and will give a witness in your spirit whether or not the idea is from Him or from satan.

STOP ROBBING PETER TO PAY PAUL

4

BREAK THE SPIRIT OF DEBT

Recognizing that debt is a spirit is the first step towards finding deliverance. We tend to think of debt as a convenience, a method of getting what we want quickly. In fact, some people will declare that they are blessed of God because of all the things they have acquired, when in reality they have been blessed by a credit card. The world has taught us to view debt in this way. However, we need to look at what God's Word says.

Financial Blessings are Conditional

We love to quote parts of Deuteronomy 28. We say we are blessed in the city, blessed in the field, blessed when we come and when we go. We are the head and not the tail, above only and never beneath. I believe that Scriptures are best understood when we consider the full context of that Word. I admonish you to get your Bible and read Deuteronomy 28 in its entirety.

Our God is a covenant God, which means He has made certain promises to us. A covenant is a mutual understanding between two or more parties, a binding agreement that promises certain benefits based on fulfillment of certain conditions. When the conditions are fulfilled, the blessings of the covenant are realized. However, inherent in the covenant are curses as well, which become the natural consequences of breaking the terms of the covenant.

Although the blessings in Deuteronomy 28 were part of the covenant God made with Moses, I believe that in Christ we have been blessed with everything that pertains

55

to life and godliness. We can enjoy these blessings in our lives because of our relationship with Christ; however, we still must meet the conditions.

Deuteronomy 28:1-2 gives the conditions of God's covenant for financial blessings. There is one small, but key word that should not be overlooked.

Deuteronomy 28:1-2
And it shall come to pass, *if* thou shalt hearken diligently unto the voice of the LORD thy God, to observe and to do all his commandments which I command thee this day, that the LORD thy God will set thee on high above all nations of the earth: And all these blessings shall come on thee, and overtake thee, *if* thou shalt hearken unto the voice of the LORD thy God.

The word "if" in these verses means that these blessings are conditional. In order to claim and participate in the blessings of verses 3-14 of this chapter, you must first fulfill the requirements. The three conditions are: to hearken diligently to the voice of God; to observe His commandments; and to do His commandments.

When we hearken diligently to the voice of God, we are listening intensely to what God says and exerting a continuous effort to make sure we are clearly hearing God's heart. To observe His commandments means that we give reverence to the Bible as the blueprint to build our lives upon; we make time to study and understand the principles of God's Word.

Finally, to do His commandments means that as we study God's Word, we allow it to change us from the inside out. Our behavior and lifestyle should become more Godly as the Word of God gets into our spirits. James 1:22 says,

"But be ye doers of the word and not hearers only, deceiving your own selves."

As we fulfill these conditions, then the blessings of God will flow in our lives. One of those blessings is that we shall be lenders and not borrowers. In Deuteronomy 28:12, it says, "The LORD shall open unto thee his good treasure, the heaven to give the rain unto thy land in his season, and to bless all the work of thine hand: and thou shalt lend unto many nations, and thou shalt not borrow."

This means that God desires to bless us so much that we will have an overflow of blessing that we can share with others. God's heart is that we would be able to operate on a cash budget and not have to borrow money.

Debt is Part of the Curse

However, there is a flip side to God's blessings, which are the curses of God. If we do not follow the conditions that are required, we will fall prey to the curses of verses 15-68. In verse 44, it says, "He shall lend to thee, and thou shalt not lend to him: he shall be the head, and thou shalt be the tail."

When you are in debt, your lender is the head over you. He can tell you to go to work whether you feel like it or not, in order to pay back your debt. He can call you on your job or call you at home to ask when you plan to pay your bill. If you don't pay, he can have you subpoenaed to a court of law so a judge can order you to pay the bill. If that doesn't work, he can even garnishee your paycheck to force you to pay the debt.

Your creditor does not care if you have a "call of God" on your life to go into full-time ministry. In fact, you may be prevented from flowing freely in your ministry calling because your head, the lender, won't allow you to quit your job.

If you are in debt, you are actually in bondage. In Proverbs 22:7 (NIV), it says, "The rich rule over the poor, and the borrower is servant to the lender." Slavery involves forced service, a loss of individual decision-making, and a loss of personal respect. You are forced to serve your master against your will. Your lender is now your lord and taskmaster. He will sometimes force you to get a second job, which will cause you to neglect your family and ministry, in order to pay back those bills. Years ago, I used to see a bumper sticker which reflected the sentiment of most debt-ridden people. It said, "I owe, I owe, so off to work I go!"

You may be thinking, "Well, why don't I just ignore these bills, allow my credit rating to go down the toilet and just go forward in ministry without ever paying my bills. Following spiritual things is more important than handling these natural things." There is a danger with this line of reasoning because it does not reflect the heart of God.

As born-again Christians, we have been made the righteousness of Christ Jesus. We are no longer wicked in God's eyes because the blood of Jesus has cleansed us. But when we choose not to pay back our bills, we are acting like the wicked. Psalms 37:21 says, "The wicked borrow and do not repay, but the righteous give generously (NIV)." Only wicked people borrow money without paying it back. But we are righteous people; therefore, we need to pay our bills even if it hurts.

I never advise anyone to file a Chapter 7 Bankruptcy. In a Chapter 7 Bankruptcy, a court of law discharges all of your debts because you can't afford to pay them. Filing bankruptcy says, "I am not going to honor the contracts that I have made. I will not be responsible for my own actions." Even though this is a legitimate law of our land, I do not believe it reflects God's desire for His people. If you are deeply in debt, I would advise you to use the plan of action that I will share with you in Chapter 8 to pay back your bills. It will require sacrifice, discipline, patience and time, but you will be a better person at the end of the process.

I am so grateful that our God is a God of mercy. In fact, His mercy is new to us every morning.   If we have missed it in terms or paying our bills in the past, we can ask God to forgive us of that sin and He will, according to I John 1:9, "If we confess our sins, he is faithful and just to forgive us our sins, and to cleanse us from all unrighteousness." But even as God forgives us and restores us to full fellowship with Him, we still must handle the consequences of our behavior.

Obedience Breaks the Curse

I remember a time when I was about to be promoted to another level in my ministry. I was excited and ready to go! However, the Lord spoke to my heart and told me that I could not go forward in my ministry until I dealt with some issues of the past. Specifically, He convicted me that there was several people whom I had offended in the past that I needed to go to individually and ask them to forgive me.

Of course, I did not want to do this! Some of these people were no longer a part of my life. I tried to reason with God saying, "What difference will this make, these people probably have forgotten all about those incidents." But God clearly let me know that if I did not obey Him in this, my ability to flow in His anointing would be limited. So I obeyed God and went to each individual to ask him or her to forgive me. This was a natural act of obedience to God but it freed me in the spiritual to flow in God's anointing more fully.

Likewise, if you desire to be all that God wants you to be, you need to obey His voice in Psalms 37:21 and go back and pay your debtors. In my business, I am often asked the question, "Won't these old debts fall off my credit report after seven years?" They are referring to the Fair Credit Reporting Act that has provisions requiring debts to be taken off a credit report after seven years. However, as a believer, we should be less concerned with our debts falling off our credit report and more concerned with obeying the voice of God. We don't obey God out of duty but because of our love for Him.

Let me point out that paying debts that you owe also includes paying back family members that you have borrowed money from. If you asked a family member for a "loan", don't act like it was a "gift". You show respect and honor for your family members by also paying them back what you have borrowed.

When you have not paid back your debts of the past, your disobedience to God's Word allows a curse to be on your finances. The spirit of bondage, debt, and poverty grip your finances. You may work harder, earn more money, get promotions on your job, buy a nicer home, but you never experience contentment in your finances.

How the Spirit of Debt Works

Several years ago, I got interested in real estate investments. I was watching television late at night and saw these infomercials declaring how you can get rich in real estate with no money down. I got hooked. Of course, they never discussed the curse of debt; in fact, they didn't even call it debt. They said I would be "highly leveraged". Didn't that sound impressive? Well, satan is a master at taking a spirit of bondage and masquerading it as a way to prosperity.

60

I began to invest in real estate. I would purchase vacant houses in the city of Detroit and rehabilitate them and then rent them out. After three or four years of collecting rents, I would sell them at a profit! I made a lot of money doing this. I made money while I rented them and when I sold them. So what was the problem? I was enormously in debt. It was difficult to get a mortgage on a house that needed rehabilitating. I was able to purchase some properties with seller financing but for the rest I used credit cards and lines of credit. At one point, I had almost $60,000 in credit card debt plus several mortgages!

Even though I had created positive cash flow and was able to pay myself a profit every month, the spirit of debt was overwhelming me. Having credit card statements coming to my house every day produced an enormous emotional strain. I was frustrated, fearful and full of anxiety. That is what the spirit of debt does to you.

God began to speak to my heart about selling all the properties. At first, I balked because I wanted to make my fortune in real estate. However, God had a better plan for my life, which I only discovered when I decided to obey Him by selling all the properties and paying off all the bills. Once the debts were paid off, it was as if a weight was lifted off my shoulders. The peace of God engulfed me in the area of my finances. I have never had a desire to get back into debt.

The Curses of the Past

We've discussed the curses that occur because of our own disobedience to God's commands. However, at times, there are curses on our finances that came from other sources.

A generational curse can occur because of the sins of your ancestors. The Bible says in Deuteronomy 5:9-10, ".... I the LORD thy God am a jealous God, visiting the iniquity of the fathers upon the children unto the third and fourth generation of them that hate me, and shewing mercy unto thousands of them that love me and keep my commandments." The actions of your great-grandparents affected your grandparents, your parents and you.

If your parents had several credit cards, were always in debt, didn't pay bills on time, and lived paycheck to paycheck, it's highly likely you are the same way. There are many people in this nation who have generational poverty, where working at a low-wage job becomes the accepted norm. I know people where the mother was on welfare and then later the daughter got on welfare. I know another family where the parents filed bankruptcy, and then as an adult, the daughter filed bankruptcy. It becomes a repetitive cycle.

Another type of curse that plagues people is a spoken curse. There is power in the words that we speak, which is why it is so important that we are careful in what we say. Sometimes, parents or teachers can speak a curse over your life by saying things like, "you will never amount to anything," or "you are just like your father."

If you are suffering from generational or spoken curses, they can be broken through the power of the blood of Jesus Christ. Galatians 3:13 tells us, "Christ hath redeemed us from the curse of the law, being made a curse for us: for it is written, Cursed is every one that hangeth on a tree." We can renounce these curses in the name of Jesus and allow the Holy Spirit and God's Word to teach us a better way.

Financial Deliverance is a Process

I like to compare financial deliverance to physical healing. We know that God is our healer and that by Jesus' stripes we were healed at Calvary. So when we have sickness in our body, we expect God to heal us. In the

Bible, we see that God healed people in a variety of ways. Some people were healed by a touch, others were healed by a word, and others were healed as they walked away.

Let's look at the story of the ten lepers in Luke 17:12 –14. "And as he entered into a certain village, there met him ten men that were lepers, which stood afar off: And they lifted up their voices, and said, Jesus, Master, have mercy on us. And when he saw them, he said unto them, Go shew yourselves unto the priests. And it came to pass, that, as they went, they were cleansed."

When it comes to physical healing, everyone is looking for a miracle. A miracle is an instantaneous manifestation of healing in our body. However, many times, God desires to heal us through a process. The process requires faith and obedience to carry it out. When Jesus told the ten lepers to go show themselves to the priests, they could have just sat there and complained because they were not instantly healed. But instead they had to have faith that Jesus could heal them and they had to be willing to obey Him.

As they began to walk, they still had leprosy on their body. Probably as they walked some distance, the leprosy was still there. However, they had a word from Jesus that they believed so they continued to go in the direction of the priests. Leprosy is a very painful disease for the body. Also, during biblical days, people with leprosy were ostracized from society. The ten lepers were walking in pain, being scorned by society, but in the midst of their disciplined effort to obey Jesus, they received the healing they desired.

Likewise, if you are in debt, you may be looking for a miracle. "I am believing God for someone to give me $50,000 so I can pay off all of my bills at one time." So, every day, you run to the mailbox looking for your "check in the mail". God may decide to bless you that way,

63

however, more than likely, He will heal your finances through a process of using a disciplined plan of action and walking by faith.

God desires to make you like pure gold. "That the trial of your faith, being much more precious than of gold that perisheth, though it be tried with fire, might be found unto praise and honour and glory at the appearing of Jesus Christ (1 Peter 1:7)."

When gold is purified, it has to go through a refining process that requires fire. The fire is not pleasant but painful. But during the process, the impurities rise to the top so they can be skimmed off. All that's left is pure gold that can be reshaped into a beautiful piece of jewelry that we will treasure. You are God's glory in the earth – that's an awesome responsibility, one that requires you to be purified, refined, reshaped. If you short-circuit the process by neglecting your bills, or filing bankruptcy to avoid your bills, you may never learn the lessons God has planned for you. But more importantly, you may never be reshaped into all that God wants you to be. God desires to prosper each of us, but He cannot pour His prosperity into a vessel that has not been purified and reshaped in order to handle the responsibilities of His blessings.

It may be painful for you and may require extreme sacrifice on your part to go back and pay all of your debts. However, in doing so, you will break the spirit of debt in your life completely and experience a spiritual breakthrough like you have never experienced before. God will promote you to another level because of your obedience to Him.

Four Steps to Financial Deliverance

The process for financial deliverance and healing involves four steps. First, you need to recognize and renounce the demonic spirits that are operating over your finances. Second, you need to commit your finances unto the Lord and seek to honor God with your money.

You can take steps one and two of this process now by confessing your faith in this prayer, "In the name of Jesus Christ, I renounce the spirit of debt and poverty on my finances. I renounce every generational curse of lack and ignorance in the name of Jesus. I am released from financial bondage by the blood of Jesus. I cancel every curse that has been spoken over my finances in the name of Jesus. I commit my finances to you, God, 100%. Teach me how to manage money. I release the spirit of discipline in my life to help me manage my finances. I thank you God, that I have been set free to receive the blessings of God in my life. I am obedient to your Word. I am a tither and a giver. I confess and forsake all sin in my life. I pay all my bills before they are due. All of my needs are met according to your riches in glory by Christ Jesus, in Jesus Name, Amen."

This prayer of faith over your finances is included in the free workbook available to you at www.StopRobbingPeter.com/workbook. It is printed in calligraphy suitable for framing. Print it out and hang it on your wall to remind you of God's blessing on your finances! The Stop Robbing Peter to Pay Paul Workbook also includes all the forms included in this book also with several bonus forms so go online now and get your free copy.

Third, develop a plan of action for getting out of debt. Make a list of all your debts including ones of the past that you have ignored. Establish priorities for paying your bills back. For example, your mortgage or rent should always be your top priority because you have to have a roof over your head. The second priority should probably be your car because you need transportation to get to and from work.

After these bills are paid, select one bill that you are targeting to pay off and put an extra amount towards that bill each month while paying a minimum payment each month to all your other creditors. Review Chapter 8 carefully for instructions on developing your plan of action.

The fourth step in financial deliverance is to be faithful and consistent in following your plan of action. It will require sacrifice, discipline and prayer. When you are trying to get out of debt, you cannot afford the luxury of eating out for lunch. Take a brown-bag lunch to work each day. Make your clothes last and only shop for necessities. For entertainment, find activities that you can do that don't cost money. For instance, taking a walk through the park, or checking out a good book from the library to read.

Pray for God to fill the void in your life that you used to fill by shopping. Depend on the Holy Spirit to help you and guide you. However, you must do the task of paying off your bills. You have to take the initiative, and then the Holy Spirit will help you. As you become faithful and consistent in handling your money, God's blessings will begin to flow in your finances.

5

THE KEY THAT UNLOCKS FINANCIAL BLESSINGS

Have you ever known a Christian who seemed to always have it together with their finances? No matter what happened with the economy, they always had more than enough to meet their needs. Even when they got news of an impending job layoff, they still praised God with exuberance. Did you wonder how they could do that? It was because they had God's blessings on their finances. When you have blessed finances, you have peace, provision, and prosperity.

God's Holy Standards

Before I explain how you can have God's blessing on your finances, I need you to fully grasp the holiness of God. From Nelson's Bible Dictionary, we learn that holy means "moral and ethical wholeness or perfection; freedom from moral evil ... Holiness may also be rendered 'sanctification' or 'godliness'. The word holy denotes that which is 'sanctified' or 'set apart' for divine service." It's important to note that only God is absolutely righteous, holy and just.

As New Testament believers, God requires that we live a holy lifestyle, "Be ye holy, for I am holy (1 Peter 1:16)." We choose to live a life that is "set apart" for God. We willingly crucify our fleshly desires as we seek to become more like Christ every day.

In His Word, God has established certain things as being holy. God had Moses separate out the tribe of Levi as holy unto Him, sanctified for Himself. They are representative of the entire firstborn of Israel, which God had already claimed for Himself when He brought the Israelites out of bondage in Egypt.

Numbers 8:14-18 (NIV)

[14]In this way you are to set the Levites apart from the other Israelites, and the Levites will be mine. [15]After you have purified the Levites and presented them as a wave offering, they are to come to do their work at the Tent of Meeting.

[16]They are the Israelites who are to be given wholly to me. I have taken them as my own in place of the firstborn, the first male offspring from every Israelite woman.

[17]Every firstborn male in Israel, whether man or animal, is mine. When I struck down all the firstborn in Egypt, I set them apart for myself.

[18]And I have taken the Levites in place of all the firstborn sons in Israel.

It's important to note that God regarded the firstborn of Israel to be holy, or set apart for Himself. As He was bringing the Israelites out of captivity, He told them to put blood on their doorposts and then the death angel would pass by their home. The Egyptians, who did not regard the God of the Israelites, did not put blood on their doorposts and so their firstborn died. However, since the Israelites obeyed God's instructions, their firstborn lived.

God gave Moses specific instructions regarding building a tabernacle where the presence of the Lord, His Shekinah glory, would dwell. The tabernacle consisted of an Outer Court, the Holy Place and the Holy of Holies.

The Ark of the Covenant was placed in the Holy of Holies, and God dwelt there between the cherubim.

The priests were only allowed to go into the Holy of Holies once a year. They had strict instructions for their own purification before entering the Holy of Holies. Also, they had to bring the blood of a slain animal to pour on the mercy seat of the ark because that was the sacrifice required to atone for the sins of the people.

Leviticus 16:2-4
²And the LORD said unto Moses, Speak unto Aaron thy brother, that he come not at all times into the holy place within the veil before the mercy seat, which is upon the ark; that he die not: for I will appear in the cloud upon the mercy seat. ³Thus shall Aaron come into the holy place: with a young bullock for a sin offering, and a ram for a burnt offering.

⁴He shall put on the holy linen coat, and he shall have the linen breeches upon his flesh, and shall be girded with a linen girdle, and with the linen mitre shall he be attired: these are holy garments; therefore shall he wash his flesh in water, and so put them on."

When the high priest followed the instructions of the Lord, he was able to successfully enter the presence of God. However, priests in those days wore bells and a rope on their robe because if they had done something wrong, they would die in the Holy of Holies. If the people outside the Holy of Holies no longer heard the bells ringing, they would pull the rope to pull the dead body out.

The Ark of the Covenant was also designated as holy to God because it was where the presence of God dwelt. Only the Levites were allowed to minister unto God in His presence. As years went on, an enemy captured the Ark of the Covenant during battle. David had recovered it, and wanted to again establish a place of worship for God. He sent people to retrieve the Ark of the Covenant. However, he neglected to follow all of God's requirements for handling the ark. David's oversight caused unfortunate results.

I Chronicles 13:7-10

[7]And they carried the ark of God in a new cart out of the house of Abinadab: and Uzza and Ahio drove the cart. [8]And David and all Israel played before God with all their might, and with singing, and with harps, and with psalteries, and with timbrels, and with cymbals, and with trumpets. [9]And when they came unto the threshing floor of Chidon, Uzza put forth his hand to hold the ark; for the oxen stumbled. [10]And the anger of the LORD was kindled against Uzza, and he smote him, because he put his hand to the ark: and there he died before God.

Uzza was probably a good man with good intentions. However, he was not a Levite. And because he was not ordained of God to touch the ark, he died while trying to keep it from falling off the cart. God is a holy God, with holy standards.

In the New Testament, God has established that communion is holy. Communion is the time when we eat bread and drink wine in order to remember the sacrificial death, burial and resurrection of our Lord and Savior Jesus Christ. The emblems we use – bread and wine – have been sanctified or set apart for communion.

Communion, therefore, is a sacred time, to be held in reverence. Paul had to give instructions to the

Corinthian church in I Corinthians 11:17-30 because apparently some people had begun to use the communion table as a time to eat dinner and get drunk. Paul warned them to eat at home and to remember the true meaning of communion. The bread represents Jesus' body that was broken for us; we were healed because of the stripes He endured. The wine represents Jesus' blood that was shed for our redemption.

Then Paul gives a strict warning that before you take communion, you should examine yourself to make sure you are not taking communion in an unworthy manner, without giving reverence to the body and blood of Jesus. Those who disregard the holiness of the communion table bring sickness and death to their own bodies. "For this cause many are weak and sickly among you, and many sleep (1 Corinthians 11:30)."

We have looked at several things that God has designated as holy: the tribe of Levi, the firstborn of Israel, the Holy of Holies, the Ark of the Covenant and the Communion table. In all of these examples, there is one common principle. When you touch that which God has decreed as holy in the wrong way, it brings about death!

The Tithe is Holy

Let's look at one more thing that God has decreed as holy. In Leviticus 27:30, it says, "And all the tithe of the land, whether of the seed of the land, or of the fruit of the tree, is the LORD's: it is holy unto the LORD." What is the tithe? The tithe represents a tenth of everything that God has blessed you with. The Israelites gave a tenth of their fruit, their herds, and their grains as a sacrifice unto God.

Since most of us are not in the field of agriculture, we give a tenth of our gross earnings unto God. We base the tithe on gross earnings and not net because Jesus said, "Render therefore unto Caesar the things which are

Caesar's; and unto God the things that are God's (Matthew 22:21)." Our gross income is our increase. We pay taxes to the government off of it and we return the tithe to God off of it as an act of faith to honor Him first in our lives.

When we ignore the principle of tithing and spend all of our money, we bring about death. We thank God that in this age of grace, we don't physically die for disrespecting the holiness of the tithe, but our disobedience does bring death to our finances. Our finances operate under the curse, which brings debt, confusion, frustration, and destruction. Your car breaks down and you can't afford to get it fixed. You always struggle with money and never get ahead. You keep trying to get out of debt yet you seem to sink further and further into debt. Why? Because your money is cursed!

Tithing becomes the key that unlocks God's blessing on your finances. I can hear some of you thinking, "Isn't the tithe part of the law? We are under grace now not the law, so why do we have to tithe?" I am so glad you asked that question because there is a lot of confusion and misinformation in the body of Christ on this issue.

Let me ask you some questions. Who lived first on the earth, Abraham or Moses? Abraham, of course. Who brought the law? Moses. So Abraham lived long before the law was in existence.

Abraham Gave Tithes

Let's look at what Abraham did after he returned from a successful battle in Genesis 14:17-20: "And the king of Sodom went out to meet him after his return from the slaughter of Chedorlaomer, and of the kings that were with him, at the valley of Shaveh, which is the king's dale. And Melchizedek king of Salem brought forth bread and wine: and he was the priest of the most high God. And he blessed him, and said, Blessed be Abram of the most high

God, possessor of heaven and earth: And blessed be the most high God, which hath delivered thine enemies into thy hand. <u>And he gave him tithes of all</u>."

Abraham gave a tithe of his spoils of war to his high priest, Melchizedek. Jacob, the grandson of Abraham, confirmed the covenant of Abraham in Genesis 28:20-22, "And Jacob vowed a vow, saying, If God will be with me, and will keep me in this way that I go, and will give me bread to eat, and raiment to put on, so that I come again to my father's house in peace; then shall the LORD be my God: And this stone, which I have set for a pillar, shall be God's house: and of all that thou shalt give me I will surely <u>give the tenth unto thee</u>."

We are Part of Abraham's Covenant

Abraham, who is called the father of many nations, had a covenant with God. In fact, his covenant was based on faith, and is an everlasting covenant that we as believers are now part of. Even though the law was abolished by grace, the faith covenant of Abraham is still in effect. And the blessings promised to Abraham's seed fall on us when we honor the covenant of faith.

Galatians 3:13-18; 29 (NIV)

[13]Christ redeemed us from the curse of the law by becoming a curse for us, for it is written: "Cursed is everyone who is hung on a tree." [14]He redeemed us in order that the blessing given to Abraham might come to the Gentiles through Christ Jesus, so that by faith we might receive the promise of the Spirit.

[15]Brothers, let me take an example from everyday life. Just as no one can set aside or add to a human covenant that has been duly established, so it is in this case. [16]The promises were spoken to

Abraham and to his seed. The Scripture does not say "and to seeds," meaning many people, but "and to your seed," meaning one person, who is Christ.

[17]What I mean is this: The law, introduced 430 years later, does not set aside the covenant previously established by God and thus do away with the promise.

[18]For if the inheritance depends on the law, then it no longer depends on a promise; but God in his grace gave it to Abraham through a promise.

[29]If you belong to Christ, then you are Abraham's seed, and heirs according to the promise.

Notice carefully that in verse 15 it says that no man can set aside or cancel the Abrahamic Covenant, it lasts forever. Even the law does not annul the promises made to Abraham and his seed in verse 17. Verse 29 lets us know that we are now Abraham's seed as believers in Christ, therefore the covenant with Abraham applies to us as well.

The tithe was established as a godly practice in the everlasting covenant of Abraham. Tithing continued during the period of the law. We know that Christ fulfilled the law and we are now living in the age of grace. But tithing continued beyond the law because Abraham's covenant continued beyond the law. Nowhere in Scripture does it say that the tithe was abolished.

In Hebrews Chapter 7, we learn that Melchizedek, the high priest of Abraham, was a type of Christ. The priesthood of Melchizedek is regarded as greater than the priesthood of the Levis (under the law) because the Levitical priesthood had limitations. Therefore, Jesus is known as "a priest forever after the order of Melchizedek (Hebrews 7:17)." Just as Abraham brought his tithe to his high priest, Melchizedek, so we need to bring our tithe to our great high priest, Jesus Christ.

Yes, we are under grace, but God is the same yesterday, today and forever more. He has always been looking for a people who will consecrate themselves unto Him and regard Him as Lord. The question to you is, "Will you allow God to be Lord over your finances?"

There is one prerequisite that you must observe before you can effectively use this key to unlock God's blessing on your finances. The requirement is for godly living. Joshua 1:8 says, "This book of the law shall not depart out of thy mouth; but thou shalt meditate therein day and night, that thou mayest observe to do according to all that is written therein: for then thou shalt make thy way prosperous, and then thou shalt have good success." Studying God's Word and obeying God's Word is a prerequisite for good success to flow in our lives.

Tithing Unlocks Heaven's Blessings

When you are obeying God's Word, then you can use the key of tithing to unlock blessed finances, or as God says in Malachi 3:7-12, you open the windows of heaven, so He can begin to pour out abundant blessings on your finances.

Malachi 3:7-12

[7]Even from the days of your fathers ye are gone away from mine ordinances, and have not kept them. Return unto me, and I will return unto you, saith the LORD of hosts. But ye said, Wherein shall we return?

[8]Will a man rob God? Yet ye have robbed me. But ye say, Wherein have we robbed thee? In tithes and offerings. [9]Ye are cursed with a curse: for ye have robbed me, even this whole nation.

[10]Bring ye all the tithes into the storehouse, that there may be meat in mine house, and prove me

now herewith, saith the LORD of hosts, if I will not open you the windows of heaven, and pour you out a blessing, that there shall not be room enough to receive it.

[11]And I will rebuke the devourer for your sakes, and he shall not destroy the fruits of your ground; neither shall your vine cast her fruit before the time in the field, saith the LORD of hosts.

[12]And all nations shall call you blessed: for ye shall be a delightsome land, saith the LORD of hosts.

We rob God by spending the tithe because He has declared it to be holy and consecrated unto Him. It's important to note here that you do not give the tithe to church; you return it. It belongs to God. So when you spend it, it is as if you are spending stolen money. The tithe is to be returned to the "storehouse", which refers to the place where you are receiving your spiritual nourishment, your local church. God desires for His house to be fully supported by His people.

The Blessings on Tithers

In this passage of Scripture, God declares several blessings that He will give to the tither. But before we look at the blessings to tithers, notice what God says in verse 10. He says, "prove me now herewith." In many other passages of Scripture, God says for us not to test Him. But here, God is telling us to test Him on this principle of tithing. It's as if God is saying, "I dare you to tithe and see how much I bless you!" Why don't you accept God's challenge!

When you begin to obey God in returning the tithe, first, He will open up the windows of heaven and pour out a blessing that you will not have room enough to receive.

If you look at your own home, you probably have two, maybe three doors to your home at most. But if you count the windows, you probably have 10-12 windows.

Imagine that your home is filled with water. What would be the quickest way to get all that water out of the house? If you just open the doors, it will come out very slowly. But if you open the windows, it will gush out on all sides! God has promised to the tithers that He will open the windows of heaven on your behalf. God wants you to overflow with financial blessings so that you can establish His kingdom in this earth. He wants you to have so much financial resources that you can help send evangelists around the world to bring souls into the kingdom.

Second, God says He will "rebuke the devourer for your sakes, and he shall not destroy the fruits of your ground". The devourer is satan. He is that thief referred to in John 10:10, where it says, "The thief cometh not, but for to steal, and to kill, and to destroy: I am come that they might have life, and that they might have it more abundantly." Satan desires to steal your finances and destroy your budget. When you tithe, God rebukes satan off of your finances.

In my own life, I have found this to be true. My husband and I have been faithful tithers since 1982. When my son was born, I became a stay-at-home mom for seven years. Although I had a real estate investment company that I operated from home, the income from it was sporadic. So basically, we based our budget on one income, my husband's job. Which meant we lived on a tight budget.

During this time period, we noticed that several people in our subdivision were getting new roofs put on their homes. Since all the houses in our subdivision were built at the same time, our roof was just as old as theirs. Several of my neighbors came to me lamenting about how their roof was leaking, how their bedroom furniture had been destroyed, and asking if our roof was leaking. I said, "No, my roof is not leaking." God knew that we did not have the money at that time to get our roof replaced so He rebuked the devourer from causing our roof to leak. A few years later, my husband received a nice bonus check from his job and then our roof leaked, in the garage without destroying anything. We had the money already in hand to pay for a new roof.

A third blessing to tithers is that your vine shall not cast its fruit before its time. Of course, the Israelites worked in agriculture and having their fruit destroyed before harvest was a real threat. But we work in other fields of endeavor today. This verse assures us of God's blessing on the work assignments that He has given to us to fulfill. We can fail miserably in business and ministry when we attempt to move forward in a project at the wrong time. God will bless us with wisdom to know what season of life we are in so that we don't get ahead of where God wants us to be at any particular time.

A fourth blessing to tithers is that "all nations shall call you blessed: for ye shall be a delightsome land." When you obey God's Word regarding tithing, other people will notice the blessing of God on your life. They will want to know what you are doing and will desire to be like you. You will stand out as someone with blessed finances.

A chart listing these and other blessings on those who tithe is included in the free workbook available to you at www.StopRobbingPeter.com/workbook.

Keep God First

When you return the tithe to God, it is important that you write the check for your tithe first. Some people get their paychecks, pay all their bills and then once they see they have enough money left, they write a check for

10% of the gross to their local church. There is a principle throughout Scripture called "firstfruits". Firstfruits mean that God desires the first of whatever we have. God desires for us to honor Him first as the Lord of our lives. Proverbs 3:9-10 says, "Honor the LORD with thy substance, and with the firstfruits of all thine increase: So shall thy barns be filled with plenty, and thy presses shall burst out with new wine."

God told the Israelites to give Him the first crops of their harvest, to dedicate their firstborn child unto Him and to sacrifice unto Him the firstborn of their cattle. In Exodus 22:29-30, it says, "Thou shalt not delay to offer the first of thy ripe fruits, and of thy liquors: the firstborn of thy sons shalt thou give unto me. Likewise shalt thou do with thine oxen, and with thy sheep: seven days it shall be with his dam; on the eighth day thou shalt give it me."

Jesus is the firstfruits of God the father (read I Corinthians 15:20-28). This is an awesome revelation. God is not asking us to do anything that He Himself has not done. Jesus was God's firstborn and only son. Yet He gave His firstfruits as a sacrifice for sin for us. He gave His very best in order to save us from our sins. How much more should we be motivated to give to God our very best, the firstfruits of our labor – the first 10% of our gross earnings!

When Jesus died on the cross for us, He redeemed us from sin. In other words, He purchased us back from a life controlled by the sin nature through the shedding of His own precious blood. When we return the tithe, the firstfruits of our labors, we redeem the other 90% of our money – we purchase it back from being under the curse. We bring our finances under the blessings of God. I don't know about you, but I would rather shop with 90% money that is blessed of God than to *try* to shop with 100% money that is under a curse.

STOP ROBBING PETER TO PAY PAUL

When we write our check for the tithe first, we live out that Scripture which says, "the just shall live by faith." It takes faith to write a check for your tithe *before* you calculate whether you will have enough money left over to pay your other bills. There were many times when I was a stay-at-home mom that our bills exceeded our income for the month. My husband and I could have justified to ourselves why we should not return the tithe first. We could have said that we could not afford to tithe.

But we believe in the same God who took one boy's fish sandwiches and fed over 5,000 people. If God can multiply fish and bread when it is dedicated unto Him, surely He could multiply our monthly income to cover our bills. So we would return the tithe anyway.

Then God would move supernaturally on our behalf. There were times when a company would contact my husband to do a consulting job on the side – he had not been looking for an extra project – and the extra income met our needs. There were times when his company decided to give him a bonus check even though his sales *did not* meet quota – now that's God's favor!

There were times when income from my rental properties came in at just the right time. Or I would sell a property and the profit was just the amount that we needed. I can say from experience that tithing works. God has proven His faithfulness to bless us and to meet all of our needs when we honor Him by returning the tithe first.

God desires to do the same for you. Decide today to live by faith by honoring God with the firstfruits of your income. Return the tithe to your local church where you are fed the Word of God. As you faithfully, consistently tithe unto God, He will prove His faithfulness to you. Your finances will be blessed and the devourer will have to take his hands off of your household. I dare you to do it! I double dare you to put God to the test!!

6

PREPARATION FOR PROSPERITY

Obedience

Obedience to God is a prerequisite for prosperity. Obedience is so important that our failure to obey God can prevent prosperity from flowing in our lives. In our nation, the United States, we have a democracy, which is a government where the people make the decisions through representation. However, throughout all of history, God has always desired a theocracy, where God is in charge and we obey His commands.

In the very first of the Ten Commandments God declares, "I am the Lord thy God ... thou shalt have no other gods before me (Exodus 20:2-3)." God wants you to honor Him first above any other thing in your life. You show honor to someone by obeying what he says.

When the nation of Israel asked for a king like the other nations, God was upset with them. Because it meant they had rejected God as king over their lives. Even though we live in a democracy, we still must look to God as the source of our supply and not government programs and policies. I am not suggesting by this statement, however, that we should rebel against government, because as believers we should show respect to the authorities that God allows to be in place.

Saul, the first king over Israel, lost his kingdom because of disobedience. God gave Saul specific instructions in I Samuel 15 to go and completely destroy the Amalekites, a wicked nation. God told Saul to kill the king, all the men, women, children and animals. Instead, Saul decided to spare the king's life, and keep some of the best animals supposedly to sacrifice them unto God. In response to this disobedience, God took the kingdom of Israel from Saul and gave it to David.

We learn two lessons from Saul's mistake. First, obedience is better than sacrifice (I Samuel 15:22). God did not want the Israelites to sacrifice those animals to Him. He wanted Saul's complete obedience. Likewise, God is not interested in us offering a sacrifice of praise to Him in Sunday worship services if we are not willing to obey His Word Monday through Saturday.

Second, we learn that partial obedience to God is the same as disobedience. We cannot do half of what God has told us and then expect to receive prosperity. We have to be willing to completely obey the Word of God for our lives. How can you obey God completely? Start where you are right now. Begin by reading and studying His Word on a regular basis. There are general principles taught in the Bible that God expects all believers to live by. For example, walking in love towards others, telling the truth, attending church on a regular basis, studying the Bible, forgiving people, praying to God daily, offering up praise and worship to Him.

As you begin to obey God in the general principles in His Word that He expects everyone to obey, then you can begin to sense the Holy Spirit's leading in more specific areas of your life. The Bible teaches us the role of the Holy Spirit in our lives. The Holy Spirit is our teacher and the Word promises that He will guide us in every area of our lives (John 14:26, John 16:13-14). Start each day acknowledging the Holy Spirit's presence and allow Him to guide you in your daily life.

Being in the Right Place at the Right Time

God has a specific plan and purpose for each person's life. Our responsibility is to discover His purpose and then take action to move into the center of God's will for our life. When we refuse to take the action that God requires then we shortchange God's blessing.

God may have spoken to you about changing jobs or careers, or going back to school to increase your knowledge or job skills. Yet if you decide, because of fear, laziness or complacency, to just stay in the same job, then you have prevented God's prosperity from flowing in your life. God's prosperity is designed to flow when you are in the center of His will for your life. It takes obedience, diligent effort, and a willingness to walk by faith and not by sight in order to get to that point.

I currently own a mortgage company, which God is using as a vehicle to prosper me. Before I launched my own mortgage company, I worked for other people's mortgage companies for nine years. A year before I went out on my own, I was working for a gentleman I'll call Oscar. Oscar had been a business colleague of mine at a prior company so when he started his own mortgage company, he recruited me to join him. Oscar liked me as an employee, and I liked him as a boss. I had been with him for three years and I had a good compensation package. I was comfortable and complacent.

As I was sitting at my desk doing my work one day, the Holy Spirit spoke to me in my spirit and said, "Update your resume." I said, "Why do I need to update my resume, I'm not planning to change jobs." The Holy Spirit said again, "Update your resume." Even though I did not understand why, I said, "Okay." I located the disk that had my resume on it, updated it and printed out a copy. Within a few days, Oscar called me into his office and said that his company was not doing well. He was going to have to cut my compensation by 30 percent! In addition, he was planning to bring on a partner to help his cash flow. I immediately received a check in my spirit regarding this partner, but I did not know why.

I found another job that I felt the Holy Spirit was leading me to and began working there within a month. After being at this new company for several months, I realized that I absolutely hated the place. The managers talked down to us; the copiers and fax machines kept breaking down; and the promised income stream was not materializing. I wondered if I had totally missed God.

One day as I was sitting there aggravated, I reflected on the five jobs I had had in the mortgage industry over nine years. I had left each job when I felt I could no longer grow or learn there. I listed out the strengths and weaknesses of each company along with the knowledge, skills, and abilities that I had gained in each place.

I realized that God had been assembling a puzzle in my life. Each company had supplied a missing piece. As I sat there confused as to why God would bring me to such a frustrating work environment, the Holy Spirit spoke to me and said, "It's so that you will know that the only place left for you to go now is to start your own mortgage company."

At that moment, it was as if the Spirit of God engulfed me. I felt the spirit of wisdom and understanding, the spirit of counsel and might, and the spirit of knowledge and the fear of the Lord. I felt a spirit of entrepreneurship come upon me. I sat at my desk and began to scribble notes on a pad. These notes later transformed into my business plan.

Over the next ten days, I slept very little, because I was on a mission. I spent time at the library researching how to incorporate a business without an attorney, and how to write a successful business plan. I went on the Internet and got the forms I needed to apply for my mortgage broker license from the state of Michigan.

Within ten days, I had written my business plan, incorporated the business, issued corporate stock, opened a corporate bank account, held my first board of directors and stockholders meetings, and submitted my 38-page broker license application to the state. I began to plan the organizational structure of the corporation, and develop my marketing plan. Throughout this process, satan tried to stop me with fear at every turn, but I pressed on.

I remember when I finally got my license approval after four months of waiting and I had to start shopping for office furniture and office supplies. Although I started with a small office, furnishings, equipment, and supplies were expensive. As I walked down the aisle of the office supply store, filling up the basket with what I needed, my stomach was doing back flips. Satan kept whispering in my ear, "You are going to lose your shirt." By faith, I kept pushing the shopping cart forward.

God gave me a word for my business, which became my strength and motivation during the difficult start-up phase. It was from Jeremiah 29:11 in the NIV, "For I know the plans I have for you, declares the LORD, plans to prosper you and not to harm you, plans to give you hope and a future." I quoted this verse whenever satan tried to stop me with fear. Once my office was set up, I printed this verse out, framed it, and hung it on the wall so I could see it every day.

Within ninety days of launching my mortgage company, Victory Financial Corporation, I had cleared all of my start-up expenses and had turned a profit. I have not looked back since. God has blessed me tremendously through this venture.

And remember Oscar, the gentleman I worked for before going out on my own? Well, after I started my company, I began to hear from people in the industry that they suspected the partner Oscar brought on to save his company was not very ethical. Over the next several months, more and more details surfaced until his company ended up being dissolved to avoid some ugly legal problems. I was so glad that I was not working for him when all of this happened!

But what if I had ignored the voice of the Holy Spirit telling me to update my resume because I was comfortable? Or what if I listened to satan's fears and refused to start my own business? I would not have been in the place where God wanted me to be at the time I needed to be there. I had to choose to obey God, in spite of my fears, in order to get to the place where He wanted me to be. Now that I am there, His prosperity can freely flow in my life.

What about you? Where does God want you to be? I urge you to prayerfully seek God's will for your life, family relationships, job, career, and education. If God is telling you to start your own business, then do the research, get the experience, and go for it! If He is telling you to seek a promotion on your job, then apply for that next level of responsibility. If God is telling you to launch into a full-time ministry position, then that is where He will bless you. Do what God is telling you to do and the blessings will follow!

Giving Produces Results

When you give offerings, you are planting seeds. Any farmer will tell you that when you plant seeds, they produce a harvest. One sure way to release God's prosperity in your life is to become a giver. When we give offerings, it is above and beyond the tithe. You need to give offerings to your local church, other worthwhile ministries and other people as the Holy Spirit directs.

The blessing to those who give is in Luke 6:38, "Give, and it shall be given unto you; good measure, pressed down, and shaken together, and running over, shall men give into your bosom. For with the same measure that ye mete withal it shall be measured to you again."

Preparation for Prosperity

This Scripture says that when you give to others, people are going to give to you. And when you receive the harvest, it is going to be an abundant amount, so much so that it will overflow in your life. It also says that whatever measurement is used for giving is the same type of measurement that will be used for the harvest. So, if you are stingy in giving, you will receive stingy harvests. However, if you are generous in giving, then you can expect generous harvests.

When I reflect on my own life, my husband and I have been givers for a long time. As the Holy Spirit has directed us, we have given offerings to our church, other local and worldwide ministries, and to people. We've given away money, clothing, furniture, microwaves, and even two automobiles.

I don't mention the things we've given away to brag but simply to say it's amazing what you can give away when you allow the Holy Spirit to lead you. I've never had a garage sale; I'd rather bless someone with the things that I no longer need that are still useful. When you give to others, you show the love of God by helping to meet the real needs of people's lives.

As I'm writing this, I look around my house at all the things that were given to us free of charge over the years. I see an exercise bike, a rowing machine, luggage, jewelry, small appliances, a pool table, and even a 61" television. We've received things from other people and also through my husband's job. The point is that God's Word works! Because we are consistent givers, people give to us as well.

Sometimes even total strangers give to me. I was walking through the lobby of an office building around Christmas time. A lady who I didn't know was making a Christmas tree out of poinsettia plants on a special stand. As she was unpacking the plants, she noticed that two plants were not poinsettias; they looked like a form of violets. She looked at me as I was just passing through the lobby, and said, "Would you like two plants?" I asked, "Free of charge?" She said, "Yes, you can have them." I said, "Thank you," and took home two beautiful plants to decorate my home.

On another occasion, I was purchasing several items at a department store. The sales clerk who I did not know looked at me and said, "I cannot, in clear conscience, sell you these items for full price today because they are going on sale in three days. So why don't I just give you 40% off of everything today?" I said, "That sounds great to me!" These may seem like small things, but I thank God for every blessing, big or small.

Servant Attitude

How do we serve others? By putting their needs above our own. Motivational speaker, and born-again Christian Zig Ziglar often says, "You can have everything in life you want if you help enough other people get what they want." This is a powerful concept that works. The most successful people and businesses are those that provide excellent service to meet the needs of others.

Jesus is the prime example of someone who came to serve others. As He observed the needs of the crowd, He was moved with compassion to minister to those needs. Jesus came to fulfill His purpose in the earth which is stated in Luke 4:18-19, "The Spirit of the Lord is upon me, because he hath anointed me to preach the gospel to the poor; he hath sent me to heal the brokenhearted, to preach deliverance to the captives, and recovering of sight to the blind, to set at liberty them that are bruised, to preach the acceptable year of the Lord." Everywhere Jesus went, He used His anointing to heal the sick, raise the dead, cast out demons, forgive sins and teach people how to live a life of victory and peace.

Likewise, each of us has been blessed with certain gifts and talents. Those abilities were not given to us for our own enjoyment but rather to bless the lives of others. In a society that seems to always ask, "what's in it for me?", it takes true humility to use your gifts and talents to serve and meet the needs of others. But those who prosper have embraced this principle. We each have something that someone else needs. You may have the gift of mercy that I need to partake of. I have the gift of teaching that I am using to bless you.

Jesus summed up the qualities of true leadership and greatness in Matthew 20:25-28, "But Jesus called them unto him, and said, Ye know that the princes of the Gentiles exercise dominion over them, and they that are great exercise authority upon them. But it shall not be so among you: but whosoever will be great among you, let him be your minister; and whosoever will be chief among you, let him be your servant: even as the Son of man came not to be ministered unto, but to minister, and to give his life a ransom for many."

Learn to live your life serving the needs of others with your giftedness. When you do so, you will find true contentment and in turn, your life will be blessed.

Faithfulness

A person who is faithful is someone who is loyal, reliable, and consistent over time. God expects us to be faithful if we are to receive our prosperity. Proverbs 28:20 (NIV) says, "A faithful man will be richly blessed, but one eager to get rich will not go unpunished." When we are faithful, we work hard on our God-given purpose on a regular basis, day-end and day-out. We cannot be double-minded. A double-minded person is someone who trusts

God today and then tries to make it on their own power and reasoning ability tomorrow. We cannot waver in our faith in God or our service to God and mankind.

As I said in the introduction to this book, we live in an instant society. We've been programmed to expect immediate results. When we take this worldly thinking into our relationship with God, we get into trouble. God is not governed by our watches and timetables. He is governed by His sovereignty. He is governed by the seasons of our lives. "To every thing there is a season, and a time to every purpose under the heaven (Ecclesiastes 3:1)." If things are not progressing in your life and finances as you would expect them to, then you need to get on your face before God to inquire from Him as to what season you are in. Seek His direction and then be faithful in obeying Him.

There are many people in the Bible that showed their faithfulness to God over long periods of time before they received their promises. God promised Abraham a son and Isaac was born 25 years later. Moses was called as the deliverer of the nation of Israel but he had to spend 40 years in the land of Midian being prepared by God before he could lead the people out of Egypt. Paul was called into ministry and then spent 17 years in preparation before he went forth to preach the gospel.

God has made many promises over each of our lives. But it will take time before we receive the full manifestation of those promises. In our time of waiting, we need to have faith that is unwavering and continue to faithfully serve God and minister to the needs of others. We cannot give up or give in to the world's way of doing things. We have to believe God's Word, "And let us not be weary in well doing: for in due season we shall reap, if we faint not (Galatians 6:9)." We will receive the promise in "due season", based on God's timetable, not ours. Our responsibility is to continue to be faithful while we wait.

Section Two

Budget

Suppose one of you wants to build a tower. Will he not first sit down and estimate the cost to see if he has enough money to complete it? For if he lays the foundation and is not able to finish it, everyone who sees it will ridicule him, saying, 'This fellow began to build and was not able to finish.'

Luke 14:28-30 (NIV)

7

Pain Free Budgeting

Up until now, I have given you spiritual principles to guide the use of your finances. Now it's time to add practical application to those principles to show you how to have financial victory. I know a lot of people get emotionally charged when managing money. So, as we begin our study on setting up a household budget, I need to remind you that "budget" is not a four-letter word! Calm down, take a deep breath and let's take the pain out of household budgeting.

Where Are You Now?

Before you can effectively put new strategies in place to help your budget, you need to first evaluate where you are right now. What are your current spending habits? Do you shop compulsively? Where is the waste in your budget? Everyone has some waste. Can you list all your income over the past 30 days and what it was spent on?

If you have difficulty answering these questions, it's time to take inventory. For the next 30 days, make a list of everything that you purchase, whether you pay for it by cash, check or credit card. You can use the Spending Inventory form for this purpose. Make extra copies of the form and carry it with you in your pocket or purse to record every expense.

Although this will be a challenging exercise, it will be incredibly enlightening. When you add up your expenses, you may find you're spending excess money on specialty coffee or eating lunch out every day. My own Spending Inventory showed I was spending a lot of money on magazine subscriptions that I didn't have time to read.

Spending Inventory

Where is your treasure (Matt. 6:19-21)? Keep an inventory for 30 days to find out where your money is currently going.

DATE	ITEM	AMOUNT	CASH/ CREDIT

Once you have completed the Spending Inventory, you will have an idea of your current spending habits. It will help you to know what items you regularly spend money on and whether you tend to spend money more by cash or credit.

You will also be able to determine whether there are certain times of the month that cause you to spend more money. If you are a person who lives paycheck to paycheck, then you will see a surge of expenses on pay day and the few days after it, then it will taper off to nothing because you have run out of money.

When you analyze the Spending Inventory, you can determine where the waste is in your budget. This information will be useful as you make decisions for your new budget. For ease in photocopying, an 8 ½ X 11 inch version of the Spending Inventory is provided in the free workbook available at StopRobbingPeter.com/workbook.

How Much Are You Worth?

The next item that you need to complete in order to determine where you are right now is a Net Worth Statement. A Net Worth Statement lists all of your assets, which is everything that you own, subtracts all of your liabilities, which is everyone that you owe, to determine your net worth.

A Net Worth Statement measures your level of wealth. When a person's net worth exceeds $1 million, they are declared a millionaire. Actually, if you were to add up your earnings over your lifetime, you will probably have over $1 million flow through your hands. The question is how much of it will you be able to convert to wealth. Net worth indicates how much of your earnings you have been able to keep.

Complete the Net Worth Statement today and again once a year to track if your financial situation is improving.

Net Worth Statement

Assets (Market Values):
    Savings Account   _____
    Checking Account   _____
    Real Estate   _____
    Investment Accounts   _____
    Pensions/401K (vested amount)   _____
    Life Insurance (cash value)   _____
    Automobiles   _____

                                  _____
    Household Furnishings   _____
    Other Assets   _____

                                  _____

         TOTAL ASSETS: _____

Liabilities:
    Mortgage   _____

    Car Loans   _____

    Charge Cards   _____

                                  _____

    Other Debts   _____

    TOTAL LIABILITIES: _____

Total Assets – Total Liabilities = NET WORTH:

                                  ========

When you complete your Net Worth Statement, do not be discouraged if your net worth is low. Remember, this is your starting point. With faith in God, hard work and diligence in budgeting, you will find your net worth increasing as the years progress.

If you completed the Net Worth Statement and found that your net worth is negative, this is a red flag! It indicates that if you were to sell everything that you have, you still would not have enough to pay off all of your creditors. Don't despair; you will probably need to take some aggressive measures in order to pay back your bills. Read Chapter 8 on Debt Busting Strategies carefully and follow the plan of action for getting out of debt.

Set Financial Goals

Before we get to the task of setting up a budget, you need to decide what you want to accomplish with your financial resources. When you set financial goals, it gives focus and purpose to your income. Your desire is not just to pay current bills but also to make progress towards your goals.

In setting financial goals, you should set goals in two categories: short-term goals and long-term goals. A short-term goal is anything you would like to accomplish in the next three to five years. Examples of typical short-term financial goals are: get out of debt; set up an emergency nest egg; go on a nice vacation; save the down payment to purchase a home, or save to remodel your existing home.

A long-term goal is anything you want to accomplish that will take you longer than five years to do. Examples of long-term financial goals are: college education for your children, retirement, or start-up capital for a business venture.

When you set financial goals, it's important to do your research to find out how much money you will need to reach your goal. Divide that amount by the number of months you have to reach the goal and then include that amount in your monthly budget for savings towards that goal.

Setting financial goals is a discipline that you should learn and also teach to your children as well. When my son, Dante, was 11 years old, he wanted more money than I was willing to give him for an allowance, so he decided to get a paper route to earn some extra cash. Of course, his objective was to use his earnings to buy every available video game and designer gym shoe he could find, so I had to put him on a budget!

He was only allowed to spend 40% of his money on what he wanted. He was required to return the tithe of 10% to church, and save the remaining 50% in his bank account. He set a goal for his savings – he wanted to buy a car when he got his license at age 16.

He kept the paper route for two years and then he got a job as a caddy at the local country club. He was earning a lot more money as a caddy, but I kept him on the same budget. By the time he was 16, he had enough money in his savings account to pay 40% of the cost of a nice used car. We loaned him the other 60% and set him up on a payment plan to pay us back at 0% interest.

Dante was incredibly proud of himself. He told all of his friends and teachers how he saved his money and bought himself a car. Not only did he get what he wanted but also he learned a lifetime lesson about the value of setting a goal and then disciplining himself to save to reach that goal.

When Dante gave up the paper route, my daughter, Tiffany, took over the route at the age of 10. I put her on the same budget. Now she's saving for a car at age 16. I am confident she will reach her goal as well.

Budgeting Basics

A budget is simply a written plan of action for the use of your finances. Rather than earn money and spend it just to pay current bills, a budget will give direction and focus to your finances. When you set up a budget, you make decisions about what you want your money to accomplish.

In order to set up a budget, you will need the following tools. The Budget Worksheet is on the pages to follow; get the other items at any office supply store.

- Budget Worksheet
- Expanding Wallet File with single section
- Expanding Wallet File with multiple sections
- Ledger Book or Computer Software

I have provided three different Budget Worksheets – A Monthly Budget, A Bi-Weekly Budget, and a Weekly Budget. The worksheet that you use is dependent upon how frequently you are paid by your employer. If you get paid each week, then use a Weekly Budget. If you get paid bi-weekly or semi-monthly, then use the Bi-Weekly Budget. All of these budgeting worksheets have been expanded to 8 ½ X 11 inch size in the free workbook available to you. Download your copy today at www.StopRobbingPeter.com/workbook.

In my household, I use the Monthly Budget. That's because when I first got married, my husband's job only paid him once a month and my income was so low it didn't pay too many bills, so I learned to pay bills once a month.

Use the Budget Worksheet to list all income and bills. It includes space for fixed and variable expenses. With the weekly and bi-weekly budget, you must decide which bills will be paid from which check based upon the amount of the bill and its due date.

Monthly Budget

INCOME	AMOUNT
Your Gross Salary	
Your Spouse's Gross Salary	
Commissions/Bonuses	
Tips	
Dividends	
Rental Property Income	
Social Security	
Pension Benefits	
Other	
TOTAL INCOME:	
EXPENSES:	
Tithes (10% of gross)	
Offerings	
Taxes & Withholdings	
Savings	
Short-term goals	
Long-term goals	
House	
Mortgage/Rent	
Insurance	
Taxes	
Maintenance	
Insurance	
Medical	
Life	
Disability	
Transportation	

PAIN FREE BUDGETING

Car note	
Insurance	
Maintenance	
Household Expenses	
Groceries	
Gas	
Electric	
Telephone	
Water	
Cable	
Charge Cards	
Personal Expenses	
Medical Doctors	
Personal/Pocket Money	
Clothing	
Entertainment	
Gifts	
Other	
TOTAL EXPENSES:	

Bi-Weekly Budget

INCOME	1ST PAY	2ND PAY
Your Gross Salary		
Your Spouse's Gross Salary		
Commissions/Bonuses		
Tips		
Dividends		
Rental Property Income		
Social Security		
Pension Benefits		
Other		
TOTAL INCOME:		
EXPENSES:		
Tithes (10% of gross)		
Offerings		
Taxes & Withholdings		
Savings		
Short-term goals		
Long-term goals		
House		
Mortgage/Rent		
Insurance		
Taxes		
Maintenance		
Insurance		
Medical		
Life		
Disability		

PAIN FREE BUDGETING

Transportation		
Car note		
Insurance		
Maintenance		
Household Expenses		
Groceries		
Gas		
Electric		
Telephone		
Water		
Cable		
Charge Cards		
Personal Expenses		
Medical Doctors		
Personal/Pocket Money		
Clothing		
Entertainment		
Gifts		
Other		
TOTAL EXPENSES:		

Weekly Budget

INCOME	1ST WK	2ND WK	3RD WK	4TH WK
Your Gross Salary				
Your Spouse's Gross Salary				
Comm./Bonuses				
Tips				
Dividends				
Rental Property				
Social Security				
Pension Benefits				
Other				
TOTAL INCOME:				
EXPENSES:				
Tithes (10% gross)				
Offerings				
Taxes & Withholdings				
Savings				
S-T Goals				
L-Term goals				
House				
Mortgage/Rent				
Insurance				
Taxes				
Maintenance				

PAIN FREE BUDGETING

Insurance				
Medical				
Life				
Disability				
Transportation				
Car note				
Insurance				
Maintenance				
Household Expenses				
Groceries				
Gas				
Electric				
Telephone				
Water				
Cable				
Charge Cards				
Personal Expenses				
Medical Drs				
Personal $				
Clothing				
Entertainment				
Gifts				
Other				
TOTAL EXPENSES:				

Decide on a Budget Day

Set up a "budget day". If you are using a weekly or bi-weekly budget, you may decide that payday is your "budget day".

If you are on a monthly budget, you decide which day you want to pay all your bills, taking into consideration when your major bills are due such as your mortgage and car note. Generally, most mortgages are due on the first of the month but allow you a grace period to pay up to the 15th of the month without a late fee. If you, like my husband, are paid on the 30th of the month, you can set your "budget day" as the 1st or the 5th of the following month.

In order to make a monthly budget work, you may need to call some of your other creditors and ask them to change the due date of your bills. Ask for a due date that is 7-10 days after your "budget day" to allow for mail delivery. Credit card companies will usually comply with this request especially when you tell them that changing the due date is the only way to ensure that you can pay them on time each month.

When bills come in the mail, they are to be placed in the single section Expanding Wallet File. You can open the envelope and glance at the bill to make sure it's accurate, and then put it into the single section Expanding Wallet File and forget about it until "budget day". It is important to discipline yourself to deal with your bills only on "budget day".

If you are deeply in debt and stressed out about your bills, having a designated "budget day" will increase your peace of mind. Stop allowing your mind to obsess about bills every day. Worrying will not pay off your bills; it will only make your miserable! Train your mind and emotions to only focus on money on "budget day". This will work wonders for alleviating stress.

PAIN FREE BUDGETING

There was a time in my life when I had over $60,000 in credit card debt. Looking at those statements as they came to my house every day began to stress me out. So I stopped opening the envelopes. I knew how much debt I was in. I knew I had to take some aggressive measures in order to get out of debt. But being stressed out and irritable was not helping me.

I began to place the unopened envelopes for my bills in the single section Expanding Wallet File as they arrived in the mail. On "budget day", I would open the envelopes and pay the bills. I may have been stressed out on "budget day", but the rest of the days of the month, I was at peace.

If you are deeply in debt, you may want to use the same strategy. After all, don't you know what the gas bill is by the envelope? Can't you identify those credit card statements before you open up the bill?

On "budget day", you take all bills out of the single section Expanding Wallet File and pay them according to your budget. This is also a good day to compare where you are with your written budget and your financial goals.

The multiple sections Expanding Wallet File is used to file bills for the current year after they have been paid. Put labels on each section of the file to cover budgeting areas. The labels I have on my file are: Bank Statements, Charitable Contributions, Credit Card Receipts, Car Expenses, Insurance Records, Mortgage, Telephone, Taxes, Utilities and Miscellaneous. Manila file folders and a file cabinet can be used in place of the multiple sections Expanding Wallet File as well.

At yearend, you have neatly filed all of your receipts and statements that you may need for preparation of your income tax return. After I take out the items needed for tax purposes, I bundle everything else up in a big rubber band, put a note on it to designate the year and file it with my permanent records in a large storage box.

Set up a Record-Keeping System

After you have paid your bills each month, it's important to keep good records of what you have spent. Invest in a ledger book where you can record manually your total income and expenses each month. There is something about writing things down that brings focus and clarity to the situation. When you record each month how much you are spending on credit cards, it will help you to see patterns in your spending habits.

In the early years of our marriage, my husband and I would pay $100-200 a month on our charge card statement. I thought that was good. The problem, though, was that we were charging $100-200 each month as well. So we were just treading water. Because I was recording our income and expenses, I noticed this pattern. Once you can identify the pattern, it can motivate you to make a change.

If you are computer-literate, I highly recommend that you explore the many different computer software options that are available that will allow you to track your income and expenses on your home computer. Once you get used to the software, it can be a tremendous time saver.

With the software that I use, the computer screen looks just like a checkbook register, so it is very user friendly. It allows me to save regular transactions such as my mortgage, car note and utilities so I don't have to retype those items each month. I can also set up classifications in order to categorize my expenses. I can classify an expense as home maintenance, medical, charity, etc.

Then, because all of the data is stored on the computer, I can print out reports that help me evaluate my spending habits, such as a cash flow report or a profit and loss report. I can also create a visual representation of my spending through pie charts or bar graphs. If I want to know how much money I spent last year on a specific category, like entertainment, I can do a search for that and instantly know the answer. I can also set up my budget on the computer and compare my actual expenses to my budget.

In essence, using a computer program to manage your household budget helps you to run your household like a mini-company. As stewards of the resources God has provided to us, good record keeping helps us answer the question, where did all my income go?

Special Note to Married Couples

I can't tell you how many married couples I have met with in my business who have separate bank accounts. Or who have totally separate credit files. One time I met with a couple where the wife literally asked her husband to leave the room so she could tell me her credit card bills because he had no idea how much debt she was in and she did not want him to know.

On another occasion, a man wanted his wife to leave the room because she didn't know how much he earned and he did not want her to find out. This type of secrecy regarding money is not good for your budget or your marriage.

Because money tends to be an explosive issue, some couples have decided to not deal with it by keeping everything separate. And they are frustrated because they can't ever seem to get ahead. You are more likely to have considerable waste in your budget when there is no accountability. Although it may be difficult at times to discuss money with your spouse, you need to open the lines of communication so you can set joint financial goals for your household.

If you want your household to move ahead financially, you need to pool your resources and become accountable to one another. Get rid of the "secret accounts", "mad money" and "my stash" and learn to work together. Realize that you each will probably have different money personalities. One may be a saver while the other person is a spender. As much as the budget allows, make allowances for these differences in personality. Learn to respect each other's opinion and not just think that your way is the "right" way. Learn what it means to compromise. It can't always be your way.

The person who should handle the budgeting and paying of bills should be whoever is most skillful at it, whether the man or the woman. If neither one of you has a particular gifting in this area, then ask yourselves who is willing to study and learn the skills necessary to do the job. A good indication is which one of you is reading this book right now!

It is important to note that whoever is placed in charge of handling the budget has to keep the other partner informed about where the money is going. Make decisions for all large purchases jointly. Each person should be given a certain amount of "personal money" that they can spend as he or she pleases without questions or receipts. However, when you are on a tight budget and trying to get out of debt, personal money may have to be limited or sacrificed.

Practical Budgeting Suggestions

There are many practical things you can do to motivate yourself to stick with a budget. Below are just a few ideas. See how many additional strategies you can come up with to reach your financial goals.

- **Evaluate your current banking relationship**. Are you paying monthly fees? If so, shop for a bank that will allow you to open a no-fee checking account. Some banks offer no-fee checking simply for having your payroll check direct deposited.

- **Buy your next automobile rather than leasing**. Studies have shown that although it may be cheaper to get into a vehicle upfront with a lease, over the long term, buying is cheaper. Buy a high quality vehicle and keep it at least seven years. Once the loan is paid off, you can use what you were paying for a car note for savings or other financial goals.

- **Limit credit card usage to one card**. I recommend having a MasterCard or Visa to use for convenience rather than carrying cash, and for emergencies. Never charge more in one month than you can afford to pay back when the statement arrives.

- **Check the interest rate and fees on your credit card.** Get a credit card with the lowest interest rate and fees that you can qualify for if you are paying off a balance. If you pay your bill in full each month, make sure you get a card with no annual fee and a grace period of at least 25 days. Compare the fees your credit card company charges as well. Many companies charge late fees, over-the-limit fees, and transaction fees for cash advances and balance transfers. They promise a low interest rate, but the fees are exorbitant. Also, some cards hike up the interest rate if you pay late; the rate may increase to 30% or more. *Read the fine print.*

- **Set limits on your personal/pocket money.** Make a decision on how much money you will have for personal/pocket money per budget period. Make your determination based on how much money you need for personal expenses, an occasional lunch eaten out, etc. Once you have run out of personal/pocket money, you simply stop spending, period! Do not go the ATM for more cash. Learn to tell yourself no.

- **Review your telephone options.** Often times, we have signed up for a lot of options on our telephone that we don't need or use. Review your phone bill to see if some options can be eliminated. Also, check with the telephone company to compare their package of services to see if switching options will save you money.

- **Set limits on the use of ATM and debit cards.** Set a daily limit or a weekly limit. Without limits, your money will just fly out the window and you will wonder where it all went.

- **Clip coupons for the grocery store.** I have saved $50-$60 a month clipping coupons. This savings can be used to pay a bill or increase my savings. It would take me about an hour to clip the coupons. Since my hourly rate on my job at the time was less than $50-60, I figured I was getting a pay raise!

- **Have your paycheck direct deposited.** The worst thing you can do is to cash your check and get all cash in your hand. You will "feel" rich and spend money compulsively. If you have it direct deposited, then you can stick with your "budget day" and write checks to pay your bills and save for your future.

- **Set limits for clothing shopping**. Buying clothing is one of the biggest budget busters. Shop for clothes at the end of the season, at discount stores or even at second-hand stores in order to stay within your budget. If you are on a tight budget, don't even go to the mall or open the sales catalogs so you won't be tempted to buy something compulsively.

- **Comparison shop major expenses.** When it's time to renew your homeowners or automobile insurance, don't just pay the bill, call around to make sure you are still getting a good rate. When you want to do major home improvements, make sure you get three estimates.

- **Avoid unnecessary insurance.** Accidental Death Insurance is a complete waste of money. Once you have adequate life insurance, your heirs will not need more benefits simply because you die in an accident.

- **Avoid extended warranties.** If a product you purchase is poorly constructed, it will generally surface during the initial warranty period. Extended warranties are a huge source of profit for retailers and a huge waste of money for consumers.

- **Increase the deductible on your insurance.** Increasing the deductible on your homeowners and automobile insurance will save you money. Make sure the deductible you select is an amount that you can easily come up with in an emergency.

- **Use one insurance company if possible.** If you insure both your home and auto with the same company, you can usually get a discount.

- **Get a part-time job.** If you are seriously over-extended in your budget, you may want to consider increasing your income with a part-time job until you can get your bills under control. Target the extra income exclusively for paying off bills and do not incur any new bills. Learn to live within your means.

Use the ideas and strategies in this chapter to help you set up and maintain a household budget. The key to successful budgeting is to not give up! Even if you blow your budget several times in a row, if you keep working at it, you will get better and see progress. Sometimes unexpected expenses cause you to blow the budget but it's important to try to get back on track as quickly as possible.

Budgeting is not a once-and-for-all activity. At the very least, you should review your budget annually to see what changes need to be made to reflect your current situation. As your lifestyle, family, and income changes, your budget will change as well. Stay committed to living on a budget. You will be able to accomplish more of your financial goals and enjoy greater peace of mind by doing so.

8

DEBT BUSTING STRATEGIES

Under the law, God gave the Israelites specific instructions regarding debts and obligations. One of their guidelines was that all debts had to have a repayment schedule that ended in the Year of Jubilee. Jubilee was the time when all debts were paid in full or canceled so the nation had a big celebration. God still wants His people to have jubilee – a time of being completely debt-free.

Although it may be necessary to go into debt to make major purchases such as a car or home, as believers, I do not believe we should make debt a lifestyle. And even when we do have to borrow money, we should make it our goal to pay off those debts as quickly as possible. The Bible tells us in Romans 13:8a, "Owe no man anything, but to love one another." I believe this verse tells us that we should pay our bills. When we don't pay our bills, there is an emotion between the lender and ourselves other than love!

There are three types of people when it comes to debt. The first type of person is someone who is paying all their bills on time each month and thinks that debt is okay because it's convenient and they are current on all accounts. The second type of person is struggling to pay their bills each month, living from paycheck to paycheck, and trying to cope in a constant state of frustration and anxiety. The third type of person has given up on paying their bills; they are thinking of or may have already filed bankruptcy, and are allowing accounts to get further behind while the creditors are trying to track them down.

It doesn't matter which one of the above scenarios represents you, this chapter is written for you. We discussed in Chapter 4 how debt is part of the curse designed to keep the blessings of God from flowing freely in your life. It's up to you to make the decision, however, that you will turn away from debt as a lifestyle. This chapter will give you concrete ideas for getting out of debt and a specific plan of action that you can implement to make it happen.

Make Getting Out of Debt Your Top Priority

Although it is extremely easy to get into massive amounts of debt very quickly, it takes time, discipline and commitment to get out of debt. You have to make a life-changing decision that you no longer wish to be in debt because in order to get out of debt, it is going to affect every area of your life.

In Chapter 7 on budgeting, I suggested you do a Spending Inventory to find out where you are right now. The purpose of this exercise was to help you locate the waste in your budget. I believe that everyone can find $100-200 a month in wasteful spending that can be cut. You will use this additional $100-200 per month in your plan to get out of debt.

When you make getting out of debt your top priority, it affects your thinking, decision-making, and habits. If you usually walk around the mall at lunchtime and end up compulsively buying things, then you will no longer go to the mall. Instead you will take a brown-bag lunch to work or eat in the company's cafeteria.

You will begin to analyze every purchase to decide if it is really necessary. You will cut unnecessary expenses and learn to live frugally. It's important as you start your plan of action to get out of debt that you do not incur any new debts. Begin to only purchase things that you can pay for in cash.

Call All Your Creditors
And Review Your Credit Report

One of the first things you should do when you decide to become debt-free is to obtain a copy of your credit report. We will discuss in length in the next chapter how credit bureaus work and how to improve your credit rating. By getting your credit report from each of the bureaus, you will know all the debts that you have outstanding, including any collection accounts or charge-offs that you've forgotten about.

The U. S. government now requires the credit bureaus to provide a free copy of your credit report (without credit scores) once a year. Although you may see advertisements offering "free" credit reports, most are trying to sell you a service. There is only one government-mandated website where you can obtain a free credit report, at www.AnnualCreditReport.com or you can call toll-free at 877-322-8228. A fee is required for your credit scores.

After reviewing your credit report and your current account statements, you should contact your creditors if you are currently behind in your bills to let them know you intend to pay them off. Talk to them about how much you can reasonably afford to pay each month to see if they are willing to negotiate a lower monthly payment. If they do negotiate a deal with you, make sure you keep your word and send them the agreed-upon amount every month faithfully.

When you call your creditors first, they are more willing to work with you than if they have to track you down. If you are current on all your accounts, especially if you have a good payment history, you should contact your creditors as well, to ask them for a lower interest rate.

Get Out of Debt Plan of Action

The Get Out of Debt Plan of Action is a ten-step process that you can follow to become debt-free.

1.   Make a commitment to get out of debt and stick with the plan.   Set a deadline date for completion.

2.   List all debts including loans from family members.

3.   Find an extra $100-200 per month in your budget.

4.   Put debts in order of priority to pay them off. Put them in order by highest interest rate to lowest, or by lowest balance to highest.

5.   Separate debts into categories, in this order: Credit cards and lines of credit, student loans, personal debts, car loans, mortgage debt. List them on the Plan of Action.

6.   Start with bill #1 as your targeted bill. On the targeted bill, you are going to pay the minimum due plus the extra $100-200 you located in your budget. Pay only the minimum due on all other debts.

7.   Once bill #1 is paid off, target bill #2. Take everything you were paying on bill #1 plus the minimum you were paying on bill #2 and begin paying it all on bill #2 each month.

8.   Once bill #2 is paid off, repeat Step 7 with bill #3. Continue this process until all your debts are paid.

9.   Close credit card accounts as they are paid off. Keep one MasterCard or Visa account for emergency purposes only. Write a letter to close each account, and to tell them not to have their telemarketers call. If you call to request the account closed, the creditor will offer you something tempting to convince you to keep it open.

10.   During this process, you must pay cash for all purchases and not incur any new debts.

I have completed an example of the Get Out of Debt Plan of Action. When Jill Consumer starts the plan, she is paying $199 on MasterCard (the $99 minimum due plus $100 she found in her budget), plus she is paying the minimum on all other bills. Once MasterCard is paid off, she takes the $199 she was paying them and adds it to her payment to Sears so she is now paying $227 to Sears and the minimum on all other bills. She continues this process until all bills are paid in full.

Get Out of Debt Plan of Action

Name of Creditor	Balance	Min. Mth Pmt	My Pmt Amt	Int. Rate	One Year Int.	Date to be Paid Off
MasterCard	$2,463	$ 99	$199	19%	$ 467	1 yr.
Sears	563	28	227	18%	101	2 yrs.
Line of Credit	4,225	126	353	15%	633	3 yrs.
Visa	8,100	243	596	14%	1,134	4 yrs.
Car Loan	17,549	330	926	8%	603	4 yrs.
Mortgage	56,000	410	1336	8%	4,480	10 yrs.

This is my plan of action for getting out of debt. I am committed to following this plan faithfully. From this day forward, I will not incur any new debts. I will begin to live within my means, which means if I don't have the cash for something, I will not buy it. My target date to have all of my consumer debt paid off is <u>4 years from today</u>. My target date to pay off my car loan is <u>4 years from today</u>. My target date to pay off my mortgage is <u>10 years from today</u>.

<u>Today</u>   *Jill Consumer*

Date   Signature

Get Out of Debt Plan of Action

Name of Creditor	Balance	Min. Mth Pmt	My Pmt Amt	Int. Rate	One Year Int.	Date to be Paid Off

This is my plan of action for getting out of debt. I am committed to following this plan faithfully. From this day forward, I will not incur any new debts. I will begin to live within my means, which means if I don't have the cash for something, I will not buy it. My target date to have all of my consumer debt paid off is _____.
My target date to pay off my car loan is _____. My target date to pay off my mortgage is _____.

_____   _____
Date   Signature

Debt Busting Strategies

- Use windfalls (tax refunds, bonuses) to pay debts
- Get a part-time job and use all income to pay bills
- Cook meals instead of eating out at restaurants
- Take a brown bag lunch to work
- Cancel unnecessary magazine subscriptions
- Limit clothing shopping – wear what you have
- Don't go to the mall or look at mail order catalogs
- Buy generic brands instead of name brands

Get Dependable Help If You Need It

If you are deeply in debt and having a difficult time making even the minimum monthly payment on your debts, then you need to seek professional help. Look in your local phone directory or search online for the Consumer Credit Counseling Service (CCCS) in your area. CCCS is a national group of non-profit counseling agencies whose purpose is to help you pay off your bills.

Because of their reputation and experience, CCCS can sometimes negotiate with your creditors for a lower interest rate and lower monthly payment better than you can. Once the plan is in place, you will make one payment to CCCS each month and they will send out the payments to each of your individual creditors.

One word of caution in using CCCS to pay your bills – some of your creditors may report your account as repeatedly late to the credit bureaus while it is being paid through CCCS which will lower your credit rating.

Avoid Expensive Options

Avoid a Chapter 13 Bankruptcy unless you are about to lose your home to foreclosure. Under a Chapter 13 Bankruptcy, you reorganize your debts with a court-ordered plan. It can cost you more than paying the bills yourself due to attorney's fees and court trustee fees; plus it will destroy your credit rating for 10 years.

I have talked with many people over the years that have filed Chapter 13 Bankruptcy. None of them were satisfied with the outcome. Most of them entered the plan to avoid foreclosure on their home. While it delayed the foreclosure, in most instances they lost their homes anyway because the amount of the payments into the bankruptcy plan ended up being more than they could afford.

Avoid a Chapter 7 Bankruptcy at all costs. By discharging your debts, you tell future creditors that you may not pay them back. It also affects your credit rating for 10 years.

Refinance Your Home to Consolidate Debts

If you own your home and it has enough equity, you can refinance to consolidate debts and get an immediate fresh start with your finances. You must decide to close credit accounts and begin to live on a cash budget to make this a real financial change. If you are not ready to give up those credit cards, then I don't recommend this option because in the long run you will just end up in more debt.

However, if you are ready for an instant change, a mortgage refinance can immediately give you a boost in cash flow by lowering your overall monthly payments. This increased cash flow can be used to help you begin to pay for your lifestyle with cash rather than credit. Or you can use some of the new cash flow to begin your savings and investment plan.

The example that follows gives an idea of how a mortgage refinance can improve your cash flow. The interest rate and payment amounts used are for illustration purposes only and do not reflect actual rates and payments.

Debt Consolidation Example

Value of Home: $ 150,000

Current Debts:	Outstanding Balance	Monthly Payment
Mortgage (8%)	$ 56,000	$ 410
Car Loan (8%)	17,549	330
Visa (14%)	8,100	243
Line of Credit (15%)	4,225	126
MasterCard (19%)	2,463	99
Sears (18%)	563	28
Total Current Debt/ Payments	$88,900	$1,236
Closing Costs	$ 1,900	
New Mortgage Debt/ Payments	$90,800	$ 559

Monthly Savings $ 677

Benefits:
- Combine all outstanding debt into a single payment
- All interest payments are now tax deductible
- Increase monthly cash available for savings and investments

Be Persistent

Getting out of debt may take you two to five years of sacrifice and commitment but it will be well worth the effort. Keep your written Plan of Action with your budget to remind yourself of your commitment. Each time you pay off a bill, put a check mark next to it and pat yourself on the back. The key to success is to never give up on your goal to become debt-free.

The Get Out of Debt Plan of Action is one of the many forms included in the free workbook available to you online at <u>www.StopRobbingPeter.com/workbook</u>. The workbook is designed to help you implement the strategies of <u>Stop Robbing Peter to Pay Paul</u> into your life more effectively.

Stop Robbing Peter To Pay Paul

9

Build a Great Credit History

I've met so many people who have had credit issues in the past and have defined themselves as someone with "bad credit". They have attached a label to themselves or allowed creditors to give them that label and accepted it as an unchangeable fact of life.

One of the things I would like to accomplish with this book is to change people's perception of their credit history. I want to build your hope and let you know that you have the power to change your credit profile. If you have poor credit now, you can have good credit! If you already have good credit, you can have great credit! This chapter will give you concrete tools and strategies to do just that.

How Credit Bureaus Work

There are three major credit bureaus: TransUnion, Equifax, and Experian. Each one of these bureaus maintains a totally separate credit file on you. Your credit file begins to be built when you fill out your first application for credit. Once you open up an account with a creditor, they begin to report information on your account to the bureaus on a monthly basis.

Your creditor will report information such as the date the account was opened, your credit limit, your outstanding balance, your required monthly payment and most importantly your payment history. The payment history tells if your account was paid on time each month or if it was paid late. Under late payments, it shows how many times your account was paid late and how late the payment was, whether 30 days, 60 days, 90 days, 120 days or more.

If the creditor does not receive any payment on the account for a long period of time, they may decide that the account is not collectable, and they will write it off on their books in order to get a tax write off for bad debts. The account will be listed on your credit report as a charge-off. If one of your accounts has been "charged off", it does not mean that you no longer owe the debt. A balance will still be reflected on your credit file. As long as it is unpaid, it will continue to have a negative impact on your credit rating.

Your credit file will also include items of public record, such as court judgments, bankruptcy and tax liens, which have a negative impact on your credit rating. If you are ever summoned to court for not paying a debt, the subsequent court judgment will appear on your credit file. Federal, state or local tax authorities can file tax liens whenever you have failed to pay taxes when they were due.

It's important to note that even though at times the Internal Revenue Service and State taxing authorities will negotiate a payment arrangement with you for back taxes that are due, you need to ask them whether or not they will file a tax lien against you, which will harm your credit rating and may prevent you from being able to qualify for loans such as a mortgage or car loan. A bankruptcy, whether a Chapter 7 or a Chapter 13, is considered a major derogatory, and can negatively affect your credit rating for up to 10 years.

Credit Scores – What Do They Mean

Each of the three credit bureaus assigns you a number called a credit score. Because each of the bureaus has their own data file on you, the information in each file may be slightly different. While most major creditors report information to all three bureaus, some smaller creditors or collection agencies may only report their information to one bureau. This is the reason why each bureau has a different credit score for you because it is based on the information that bureau has in its file.

A credit score is a number between 350 and 900, which reflects your credit worthiness. Credit scores are used by many different industries so it is imperative for you to know your score and keep it as high as possible. Mortgage companies use credit scores to determine if you are approved for a mortgage loan and what interest rate and terms you will be offered.

Auto loan companies, credit card providers and other finance companies use credit scores to determine whether to approve your loan application.

Both life insurance and property and casualty insurance companies use credit scores to determine the amount of your insurance premiums. Many corporations are even using credit scores to determine whether or not to hire a prospective employee. Since your credit score can impact many areas of your life, it is too critical to ignore, you must work to improve or maintain it.

So what does the score mean? Although each creditor may view credit differently, the following can be considered general guidelines for evaluating your credit. Since the collapse of the sub-prime mortgage sector, many lenders have tightened their credit standards. A credit score of 720 or higher is considered excellent or "A+". A credit score of 660-719 is considered good or "A" credit. A credit score of 620-659 is considered the "A-" range, which means that your credit options are becoming limited. A credit score of 619 or below makes it increasingly difficult to get approved for credit offers.

Of course, if you have "A+" credit, you can generally qualify for loans at the best interest rate and terms available, provided you have the income and employment stability to support the loan. A person with "A" credit can probably still qualify for the best rate and terms provided they have other strong factors such as savings. When you get to the "A-" category or below, each lending institution has their own criteria for how they will evaluate your credit. Typically, the lower your score, the higher interest rate you will pay for mortgage and car loans, and you will pay higher insurance premiums or the lender may decline your application entirely.

Many employers are reluctant to hire a new employee who has a low credit score because they fear that the employee will be so stressed out about financial concerns that they will not be focused on the job; or that the employee might be tempted to embezzle money in order to pay their mounting bills.

What Determines Your Credit Score

A credit score is determined by several factors. While the developers of the credit score models will not disclose exactly how credit scores are derived, they have given us general guidelines for what determines the scores.

First, credit bureaus look at the recency of credit issues. How recent were your late payments? The most critical time period on your credit report is the past 12 months. If there are late payments within this time, they will have a more dramatic effect on your credit score, lowering your score significantly.

The second important time in your credit file is from 12-24 months. Late payments during this time period will still have some effect on your scores although it won't lower your score as much as the more recent late payments.

Late payments that occurred over 24 months ago generally have minimal impact on your credit scores.

Another factor that is considered in determining your credit score is the severity of the issues. A 30-day late payment does not have as much negative impact on your score as does a 90-day late payment. A charge-off or collection account is considered a major derogatory and will have more of a negative impact on your credit scores.

Any type of public record item, such as court judgments, tax liens or bankruptcy, are also considered a major derogatory and will cause your credit score to drop significantly. While most other negative issues including court judgments and tax liens will no longer affect your credit scores very much two years after they are paid off, a bankruptcy can continue to negatively affect your credit score for up to 10 years.

The frequency of your credit issues is also a factor that determines your credit score. How often are you late paying your bills? If you only have one late payment a year on a small retail credit card, it will have minimal effect on your credit score. However, if you routinely pay your bills late on several accounts month after month, it will have a significantly negative impact on your credit score.

Credit bureaus also consider the type of account that a late payment was made on in determining what impact that late payment will have on your credit score. For instance, your mortgage is considered the most important account on your credit report. Consequently, a late payment on a mortgage loan will have a much greater impact to your credit score than a late payment on a retail charge card. I have seen a credit score drop by 100 points due to a 30-day late on the mortgage within the past six months. I have also seen a credit score drop by over 200 points due to a 90-day late on a mortgage within the past six months.

The second most important type of account on your credit file is installment debt, such as car loans and leases, and student loans. A late payment on an installment account won't hurt your score as much as a mortgage late, but it will be damaging.

Other factors that are considered in credit scores are the number of accounts that are open and how long they have been open. Typically, if you have four open credit accounts, which could include a mortgage, car loan and two credit card accounts; and at least two of those accounts have been open for at least 24 months; it will have a positive impact on your credit score.

If, however, you have 15 open credit accounts, it will have a negative impact on your credit score. Too much access to credit will lower your credit scores. In addition, if all of your credit accounts were opened in the past six months, you will have a lower credit score, because you have not built up a long enough track record.

The number of inquiries on your credit report within the past 90 days also has an impact on your credit score. Whenever you apply for credit, the creditor pulls a copy of your credit report, which then shows up on your credit file as an inquiry. There is nothing wrong with an inquiry except if you get too many of them within a short period, it can have a negative impact on your credit.

If you have 1-5 inquiries within a 90-day period, it probably will have minimal impact on your credit score. More inquiries than that will begin to significantly lower your score. The reason that multiple inquires lowers your credit score is because when you inquiry about credit at several places in a short period of time, future creditors are concerned that you may be planning a huge shopping spree and end up enormously in debt and unable to pay back your bills.

While it's important to know what factors a credit bureau uses to determine your score, it's also important to know what factors they do not consider. Credit scores do not consider your income, where you live at, where you work or how many years you have been employed. While these are factors that any creditor will ask you on their application, the credit score does not evaluate these areas.

Improve Your Credit

There are several things you can do to improve your credit score. You should first obtain a copy of your credit report from all three credit bureaus and fix any errors that are reported.

You can contact the bureaus by phone or online:

- Experian   1-888-397-3742, www.experian.com
- Trans Union 1-800-888-4213, www.transunion.com
- Equifax   1-800-685-1111, www.equifax.com

I frequently see errors on people's credit reports. Sometimes a credit bureau will mistakenly include information on your report for family members who have similar names. Also, you may have disputed an item with a creditor and had it resolved only to find it reported inaccurately to the credit bureau. Sometimes, I see information still being listed on a credit report long after the seven years that the Fair Credit Reporting Act says it should stay on there.

You have the right to dispute any inaccurate information that is being reported about you in your credit file. First, you should contact the creditor who is reporting the information to the bureaus to see if you can get them to correct it. Make sure you ask the creditor to send you a written verification of the correction they will report to the bureaus. If you are unsuccessful in working with the creditor, then you can dispute the items directly with the credit bureaus.

Since each bureau maintains a totally separate credit file on you, it is imperative that you file a complaint with each bureau. Submit written documentation to the bureaus to support your claim. The credit bureaus will investigate your issue and report back to you within 30 days on what corrections they made to your credit file.

When you go online to get your free workbook at www.StopRobbingPeter.com/workbook, you will also get information about an ebook that I wrote on Credit Repair Made Easy. It gives you step-by-step instructions on how to repair your credit yourself and also provides a discount for a reputable credit repair service should you decide you need assistance in restoring your credit.

If you are currently behind on your bills, here is what you should do. Any debts that are currently past due but still open accounts should be brought current and then paid every month on time so that over time you can improve your credit score. *Do not just pay these bills off lump sum, as that will not help your credit rating.*

Call your creditors if you are having trouble paying your bills. If you take the initiative to call them, they are more likely to work out a payment arrangement with you. If you go into hiding and refuse to take any calls from your creditors, then they are more likely to charge you the maximum penalties, late fees, etc, which will only hurt you further.

Any accounts that are in charge-off status, collections or judgment are best paid off lump sum. For these accounts, you should call the creditors to see if they will negotiate a settlement with you. A lot of times, they will accept 50-75% of the balance due if you can pay them off lump sum.

You may be wondering how you can come up with the cash to pay these bills off lump sum. Consider these options. If you own your own home, you can possibly refinance your home, taking cash out to pay off your old bills. Make sure that if you do this that you are really ready to make a change in your spending habits because you are putting your home on the line. You don't want to end up back in debt again in two years.

Another option is to use tax refunds or bonus checks from work to pay off old bills. Resist the temptation to buy something new when you receive a lump sum of cash; instead use it to get out of debt and clean up your credit. Another idea for raising cash is to have a garage sale. Sell things that you no longer need. Use all the cash you raise to pay off old debts.

If you have minimal credit or you have had credit issues in the past, you may need to open one or two new accounts in order to rebuild your credit file. Consider applying for a gas card or a department store card, which can be easier to qualify for than a MasterCard or Visa account.

If you cannot qualify for one of these, then apply for a secured MasterCard or Visa. With a secured credit card, you would deposit an amount, say $500, into a bank account. In exchange, the financial institution will give you a credit card with a $500 limit. Once you use the credit card and begin to make on-time payments, it will improve your credit score. Be careful in applying for a secured credit card – you should not have to pay any large upfront processing fees or exorbitant annual fees. Shop around for a reasonable deal from a local bank or credit union.

Begin to use credit responsibly. Never charge more on your credit card than you can reasonably pay back in one month. Pay more on the bill than the minimum monthly payment. Most importantly, pay your bills on time every month. Late payments hurt your credit score. If you have trouble remembering to pay bills on time, set them up for automatic withdrawal from your checking account and make sure you keep enough money in your checking account to cover the automatic withdrawals.

Keep your credit usage to a minimum. There is no reason why you should need more than two or at most three credit cards. Since most retailers now accept MasterCard or Visa, I just carry one credit card. Remember that just because a company will approve you for a credit card does not mean that you should accept it. Learn to say no to excess credit – it will help both your budget and your peace of mind.

Pay all bills that come to your house before they are due, including utility payments, medical bills, insurance, cable, etc. So many people ignore medical bills thinking that their health insurance will cover it. Make a phone call to find out if your insurance is going to pay it and follow up on it. The types of bills listed above are not usually reported on your credit report; however, all of them will be listed on your credit report if they end up in collections.

Balance your checkbook regularly and avoid bouncing checks. Bounced checks are usually turned over to a collection agency that will report it to the credit bureau. Also, if you regularly bounce checks, your financial institution may close your account "with cause". Then, you may find it difficult to open another checking account at another institution.

Nearly 80 percent of financial institutions belong to the ChexSystems network, a nationwide database that tracks bank accounts closed for cause. If your checking account is closed "with cause", then your name will be listed in this database for five years. When you try to open another checking account, the new financial institution will check the database, find your name listed there and refuse to open a checking account for you.

Never Co-Sign A Loan

The Bible has two passages of Scripture that specifically speak against co-signing loans for people. In Proverbs 11:15 (NIV), it says, "He who puts up security for another will surely suffer, but whoever refuses to strike hands in pledge is safe." Proverbs 17:18 (NIV), says, "A man lacking in judgment strikes hands in pledge and puts up security for his neighbor."

Both of these Scriptures from the book of wisdom in the Bible, Proverbs, tells us that you are not exercising sound judgment when you agree to be responsible for the actions of someone else. If you co-sign a loan for someone else, you will likely bring suffering upon yourself and your family. In my business, I have met many people who have regretted their decision to co-sign a loan for a family member or friend.

Some people have the mistaken idea that as co-signor of a loan, the creditor will seek to collect the debt from the first person on the application and not them. This is not true. When you co-sign a loan application, you are just as much responsible for paying that bill as the first person.

If your friend or family member does not pay the bill on time, the creditor is going to try to collect from whoever he thinks can pay. If you have a great credit history, it will probably be you. In addition, if your friend or family member pays the account late or allows it to go to a collections account, it will ruin your credit as well. The creditor can take you to court and sue you to force you to pay the bill. He can garnishee your wages or require it to be withdrawn from your bank account.

So my advice is, don't do it! Don't co-sign that loan. After you've spent your time and energy to build a great credit history, why would you give someone else the ability to destroy it for you?

Time Heals

The main theme that is woven throughout this chapter is time. You may be able to ruin your credit quickly by paying your bills late for two or three months. However, in order to rebuild it, it will take time. Paying bills on time over time is the only key to improving your credit profile. Avoid looking for some quick fix solution to the problem. Make a decision to become more disciplined in paying your bills on time each month. Then check your credit report again at these intervals: after six months, after 12 months, after 24 months. You will see your credit score improve and through your disciplined efforts, you will see that you can build a great credit profile.

10

PLANNING FOR THE FUTURE

If you are like most people, you dream of things you would like to do in your lifetime. Making your dreams a reality, however, takes goal setting, planning, and living a disciplined lifestyle. In the financial arena, there are many possible goals – buying your first or next home, getting out of debt, buying a new car, starting a business, saving for college for your children, preparing for retirement.

The purpose of this chapter is to encourage you to set both long- and short-term financial goals and to give you basic information on various types of products and services that will help you to reach your goals. I am not giving advice on any specific investment vehicle and recommend that you consult with a qualified financial planner to develop a financial plan that will fit your particular situation.

Goal-Setting

Goals must be wise – written down, intentional, specific, and have an end date. As you begin your financial goal setting, get out pen and paper so you can write down what your goals are. Writing goals down gives a sense of formality and commitment to your goals. It also becomes a point of reference so you can read them on a regular basis to help keep you on track in your savings.

For a worksheet to help you set your financial goals, go to www.StopRobbingPeter.com/workbook to download your free Stop Robbing Peter to Pay Paul Workbook.

Set your goals intentionally, in other words, your goals should reflect your purpose in life. If you have always wanted to be an elementary school teacher yet circumstances prevented you from finishing your undergraduate degree initially, then one of your goals should be to fulfill your life's purpose of being a teacher. Your savings should be geared towards accomplishing that goal.

In order to be effective, goals need to be specific. A goal that is specific is one that is precise, definite, clearly stated and easily measured. If your goals are too vague, it will be difficult to determine whether or not you have reached them successfully. An example of a specific goal is: to save $10,000 over the next year to be used to purchase our first home. A vague goal would be: to save some money. It's difficult to measure whether this goal was accomplished.

Give your goals an end date so that you will be motivated to accomplish your goals within a certain time frame. For some financial goals, your end date is already determined for you. For instance, if your child is eight years old, you have 10 years to save for college, that's your end date. If you are 45 years old and would like to retirement at age 65, then that becomes your end date for achieving your goal. Once you have a definite end date, then you can plan your savings and activities to accomplish your goal within that time frame.

Emergency Nest Egg

One of your first goals after setting up a budget and getting out of debt should be to set up an emergency nest egg. Once you have gotten out of debt, begin to pay yourself the amount you were paying on your credit cards each month, only put the amount into a savings account.

Your goal for your emergency nest egg is to save the equivalent to three-six months of the net income for your household. If this goal seems too daunting, then set an initial goal to have at least $1000 in an emergency fund. Once you reach that goal, add to it regularly until you save the three-six months of your net income. The purpose of the emergency nest egg is to cover emergencies – those unexpected large expenses such as car and home maintenance, medical bills or a sudden job layoff.

It amazes me how many people are shocked when their car needs maintenance. Since man in a fallen world makes everything you own, it begins to deteriorate as soon as you buy it. Your car and your home are made with parts that will eventually wear out! So expect things to need maintenance, only plan for it in advance.

Once you have set up an emergency nest egg, it will increase your peace of mind tremendously. Unexpected large expenses that your budget didn't plan for will no longer sideswipe you or cause you to use your credit card. Your emergency nest egg should be kept in a savings account that is easily accessible. It should be used for emergencies only, not other expenses, such as family vacations, new clothes or luxury items. These items need to be planned for as part of your regular budget.

Life Insurance

If you have people who depend on your income to live, such as a spouse or children, then you should purchase life insurance that will replace your income if you were to die prematurely. If you are single, have no children and no one depends on your income, then you probably do not need life insurance or you may only need a basic policy to pay burial expenses and any debts that you owe.

Life insurance is used to cover your burial expenses and to set up a financial cushion to take care of your family. The amount of life insurance you purchase depends on your current income. The goal should be to provide enough insurance so your family can live off of the interest after the insurance proceeds are invested.

Without adequate life insurance proceeds, your family is left scrambling how to make ends meet financially at a time when their emotions are strained and they are ill-prepared to handle the additional pressure.

There are various types of life insurance products available. However, all policies fall into one of two basic categories: term life insurance or cash value life insurance. Term life insurance provides life insurance protection only for a specified term, which is usually renewable. Cash value life insurance combines life insurance protection with a savings plan. The savings plan component varies widely throughout the insurance industry.

Term life insurance is very inexpensive when you are young and your need for coverage is greatest due to high debts and the need to provide for young children. However, as you get older, the cost of term life insurance increases dramatically. The strategy for purchasing term life insurance is to buy the policy when you are young and healthy, then over the years, use prudent investment vehicles to build your savings and investments so that when you get older, your need for life insurance is less. This is the strategy that I use in my household.

Cash value life insurance is called by many different names, including variable life, universal life, whole life, etc. Although the cash value policy premium remains the same over the life of the policy, the premium amount is much higher than term insurance. Some cash value policies allow you to increase or decrease the amount that is contributed to the savings component. Other policies allow you to select the investment products, usually mutual funds, for your savings portion.

If you find it difficult to discipline yourself to save money, a cash value policy will provide forced savings for your household. The cash value portion of the policy can be borrowed against or withdrawn from if a need arises. However, any loans or withdrawals will be deducted from the face value of the policy when you die. Because of the high cost of cash value insurance, it is difficult to purchase adequate insurance for your family's needs using only whole life insurance.

Group life insurance is offered to employees. This is usually a term life insurance policy, which is usually limited by the benefit guidelines of that company; typically companies offer life insurance equal to the amount of your annual salary. As you will see in the Life Insurance Needs Calculator that follows, this will not be adequate life insurance for your family's needs. Also, when your employment with that company ends, so does your insurance coverage, which would leave your family unprotected.

Life Insurance Needs Calculator

In the Life Insurance Needs Calculator that follows, it asks for how much expected social security benefits your family will receive. The Social Security Administration annually sends out a benefits statement a couple months before your birthday. Use the figures on that statement to compute your family's expected benefits. If you have not received your annual statement, contact the Social Security Administration.

Refer to the benefits package of your current employer to calculate how much you can expect in pension benefits and if those benefits will be paid to your spouse after you die.

If you want your home paid off when you die, enter that amount under debts to be paid off so you have enough insurance to cover that expense. If you have savings for retirement or other life insurance such as a cash value policy, subtract that amount.

The chart that follows will help you figure out how much life insurance you need to provide for your family. I have included a completed Life Insurance Needs Calculator to give you an example of how it may turn out. Don't be surprised if you need more life insurance than you expected.

Life Insurance Needs Calculator

Total annual income to be replaced:	$ 60,000
: Minus annual social security benefits	$ 21,000
: Minus annual pension benefits	$ 18,000
INCOME SHORTAGE	$ 21,000
Divide by rate of return on conservative investment	.04
ASSETS NEEDED	$525,000
: Plus final expenses	$ 10,000
: Plus debts to pay off	$100,000
: Minus savings/other life insurance	$200,000
INSURANCE NEEDED	$435,000

Based on this example, this person should purchase a life insurance policy with a face value of $435,000 in order to adequately provide for the financial needs of his or her family after they are gone.

Life Insurance Needs Calculator

Total annual income to be replaced:	$
: Minus annual social security benefits	$
: Minus annual pension benefits	$
INCOME SHORTAGE	$
Divide by rate of return on conservative investment	.04
ASSETS NEEDED	$
: Plus final expenses	$
: Plus debts to pay off	$
: Minus savings/other life insurance	$
INSURANCE NEEDED	$

A Life Insurance Needs Calculator form that you can easily photocopy is included in the free workbook that you can download at StopRobbingPeter.com/workbook.

Disability Insurance

According to the National Underwriting Company, if you are between the ages of 35 and 65, you are twice as likely to become disabled for three months or longer than you are to die. If you become disabled and are unable to work, how will you pay for your mortgage or rent, car note and other household expenses?

Disability insurance replaces a portion of your income during the period that you are disabled, so that your household expenses can continue to be paid. These policies have various provisions, which you should discuss with your insurance advisor before determining which policy is best for your needs.

Short-Term Savings

What are your short-term financial goals? It may be to save to purchase your first or next home, or to make improvements to your existing home, or to go on a nice vacation. Whatever financial goals you would like to achieve in the next three-five years would fall under this category.

To achieve your goals, you will need to start with an accurate idea of how much your item will cost and the end date for achieving the goal. Then divide the estimated cost by the number of months until your target date. This amount needs to be put in your budget each month as savings. Set up a separate savings account for your short-term goals and write yourself a check as if it were a bill or have the amount automatically transferred every month and deposited into that account.

A money market account is an option for your savings for short-term goals. A money market account is a mutual fund that invests in the money market. It is an investment where you can get a better return than a regular savings account, while maintaining the safety of your money.

Long-Term Investing

Your long-term financial goals are for things you want to accomplish that have a target date longer than five years away. Typical long-term financial goals include saving for the college education for your children and for retirement. In order to accurately project whether you will reach your long-term goals, you need to take into account how much you are saving, what type of investment products you are using, your time frame, your income tax bracket, the projected rate of inflation, and projected rate of return on the investment vehicles utilized. Because of the complicated nature of planning for long-term financial goals, a qualified financial planner should be consulted.

There are many different types of investment vehicles available to you. Shares of stock in a company represent ownership of the company. As a shareholder, you can participate in the profits of the company through dividends paid out. A bond is a debt instrument where you are loaning money to an entity at a specified rate of return. Corporations, the federal government, and local municipalities offer bonds. When you invest in stocks and bonds, there are both risks and expected rewards involved.

Another way to invest in stocks and bonds is through the purchase of shares in a mutual fund. A mutual fund is a fund managed by a professional investment company that takes the small contributions of thousands of investors, pools it together and then purchases shares of stocks or bonds, depending on what type of fund you invest in. A mutual fund allows you to spread your money across different sectors of the economy, a process called diversification, which will reduce your risk in the market.

Estate Planning

An estate plan is a written plan to let your family know how you want your property and money divided up after you die. It can be as simple as a will, which would specify who gets what, who you want to be your personal representative to distribute your property and who you would designate to be legal guardians for your minor children should you die prematurely.

Developing a will is a very difficult thing to do emotionally – it seems no one really wants to accept his or her own mortality. We have all heard stories of families that were torn apart after a loved one died because everyone was fighting over who was to get what. Do your family a favor by putting your wishes in writing in a will. Then, go over your wishes with your family so everyone knows what to expect when that time comes.

Estate planning can be as complicated as a trust agreement if you have a lot of assets. A trust is a separate entity that is set up to take ownership of your assets, which will help your family to limit estate taxes paid to the government. An attorney who specializes in estate planning should be consulted to help you set up the appropriate plan for your situation.

Planning your estate can be a complicated process covering a lot of details. To help you better plan your estate, I developed a questionnaire to help you with the process. It is included in the free workbook available to you at www. StopRobbingPeter.com/workbook.

Section Three

Contentment

I am not saying this because I am in need, for I have learned to be content whatever the circumstances. I know what it is to be in need, and I know what it is to have plenty. I have learned the secret of being content in any and every situation, whether well fed or hungry, whether living in plenty or in want. I can do everything through him who gives me strength.

Philippians 4:11-13 (NIV)

11

Transformed Finances

In order to have transformed finances, we must take the stress out of managing our money. We can only do that with God's help and guidance. The first step, as we have learned, is a changed attitude regarding money. We need to apply God's principles to our attitudes instead of the world's ideas. Secondly, we need a written plan of action, a budget, which will guide us and keep us focused towards our financial goals. Finally, we need to learn to trust God and seek His will in every financial decision. In so doing, we find a contentment like we've never experienced before.

God has given us so much wisdom in His Word that we can apply to our lives. The book of Philippians is a book of encouragement that the Apostle Paul wrote to the Philippians to thank them for their financial support for his ministry and to let them know that because they were supporting the gospel, God would provide for their financial needs as well.

The Keys to Financial Contentment

In Philippians 4:4-7, we read some powerful Scriptures that can help us handle any stressful situation including managing money. It says, "Rejoice in the Lord alway: and again I say, rejoice. Let your moderation be known unto all men. The Lord is at hand. Be careful for nothing; but in every thing by prayer and supplication with thanksgiving let your requests be made known unto God. And the peace of God, which passeth all understanding, shall keep your hearts and minds through Christ Jesus."

These verses give us some keys to living a life of contentment in the area of our finances. The first key is to make a decision to rejoice no matter what. The Word does not say rejoice if your circumstances are what you want, or rejoice when all your bills are paid, or rejoice when you feel like it; it simply says rejoice in the Lord always. Make praise and worship of God a lifestyle. It will improve your attitude.

Sometimes we make the mistake of allowing our finances to rule us. When our income is up and the bills are paid, we are up; when our income is down and the creditors are hounding us, we are down. Our emotions become a roller coaster being ruled by our financial situation. Put God back on the throne of your life. Praise Him at all times for who He is not just when things are going well for you.

The second key is to remain calm. The Bible says, "Let your moderation be known unto all men. The Lord is at hand." According to Webster's dictionary, moderation means "avoidance of extremes, calmness." Don't allow your emotions to cause you to fly off the handle over the situation. Take a step back, take a deep breath and calm down.

One of the reasons I believe that money problems cause so many divorces is because spouses begin to blame each other when money issues happen. Don't do that – don't fix the blame, fix the problem. Blaming each other won't solve the problem, but the concrete strategies in this book will help you if you apply them.

The main reason why we should remain calm even in difficult situations is because "the Lord is at hand." He is right there with you in the midst of your trying situation. You don't have to be uptight, learn to sense God's presence and His leading in your finances and your life. He wants to meet your needs, and to bless you abundantly, but you need to be willing to submit to His way of doing things.

Transformed Finances

The third key to contentment is to get rid of worry. The Bible says to "be careful for nothing", in other words, don't worry! When you worry, you become obsessed with the negative situation. You go over and over the problem in you mind and come up with all the possible negative outcomes that may happen. Most of the time the things you imagine never occur but your emotions react as if they are fact and you find yourself stressed out, uptight and frustrated. Worry says to your mind, "I am drowning in this debt. I won't ever pay these bills off. My situation is hopeless."

Worry is particularly dangerous for a Christian because it destroys your faith. When your finances are under attack from the enemy, you need to reaffirm your faith in God's provision.

Strengthen your faith by making this confession. "God I thank you that I am on a new course with managing my finances. You are in control. I submit my finances unto You. Guide me daily in my financial decisions. I trust in Your provision because I can do all things through Christ who strengthens me. I thank you God for supplying all my needs according to Your riches in glory by Christ Jesus. I have the favor of God upon my life. I am blessed in my finances in Jesus Name."

The fourth key to financial contentment is to learn the power of prayer. Philippians 4:7 says, "...in every thing by prayer and supplication with thanksgiving let your requests be made known unto God." Prayer changes things, mostly you! When you pray, you are committing your situation to the Lord. God loves for us to depend on Him. When we do, we exchange our weakness for His strength.

When we pray to God, we bring forth angels to move on our behalf. In the natural, we must obey God by returning the tithe, giving offerings and paying our bills.

153

But when we pray during the process and commit it all to God, then He can move supernaturally on our behalf to multiply our efforts.

During the times in my life when our bills exceeded our income, I reminded myself that I serve the same God who took one boy's fish sandwiches and fed five thousand people! God can work it out for you too!

In Psalms 37:5, it says "Commit thy way unto the LORD; trust also in him; and he shall bring it to pass." We need to learn what it means to totally commit a situation to the Lord. When a person dies, the service at the gravesite is sometimes called the Committal Service. It is the time when we say our final goodbyes to the person, the casket is lowered into the ground, and we walk away and go on with our lives. We don't go back and try to get the person, because we accept the fact that the person has passed away.

We need to commit our problems to the Lord in the same way. When we come to God with a problem, we need to release it to Him totally, trusting Him to solve it. Oftentimes, we bring our problems to the Lord and then go back and pick them up again, worrying and complaining and trying to solve them ourselves.

The second half of Philippians 4:7 says, "and the peace of God, which passeth all understanding, shall keep your hearts and minds through Christ Jesus." This is the result of prayer, we can live a life of peace – in good times and bad, when we don't have enough money and when our accounts are overflowing. We learn what it truly means to walk by faith and not by sight. We learn that we can sleep peacefully at night and live a life of joy and contentment during the day because God is in control.

Control Your Thought Life

Our adversary, satan, is always trying to defeat us. One of the main strategies he uses in his arsenal is to attack our minds with thoughts of doubt, defeat and hopelessness. We need to take control of our thought life and bring it under the control of Holy Spirit who lives inside of us.

The Word of God gives us guidelines on what we should think about in Philippians 4:8, "Finally, brethren, whatsoever things are true, whatsoever things are honest, whatsoever things are just, whatsoever things are pure, whatsoever things are lovely, whatsoever things are of good report; if there be any virtue, and if there be any praise, think on these things."

We need to discipline ourselves to evaluate every thought that comes into our minds to see if it fits the criteria in this verse. For instance, it may be true that you are behind in your bills, however, since it is not a good report, you don't need to dwell on it. I didn't say you didn't need to do something about it, but you just don't need to think about it all the time and obsess about it.

In the chapter on budgeting, I suggested that you set aside specific "budget days" for dealing with your finances. When it is not the time to deal with your finances, you should not allow financial concerns to be in your thoughts. Think about other pleasant things in your life. This will increase your peace of mind.

This verse asks you to find anything in your life of virtue, in other words, anything that is good or excellent. Is there anything praiseworthy? Then focus your mind on these things. Learn to look for the good in every person and situation.

Two people can look at a glass that is partially filled with water and see different things. One person will say the glass is half empty; the other person will say it is half full. The person who sees the glass as half full has a positive expectancy; they are expecting it to become completely full. Learn to expect the best for yourself and your life. Believe that God desires to bless you.

Christ Is Our Contentment

In writing to the Philippians, Paul was excited that they had once again sent him a financial gift for his ministry. However, he made it clear that he had learned the secret of contentment in his finances.

Philippians 4:10-13

[10]But I rejoiced in the Lord greatly, that now at the last your care of me hath flourished again; wherein ye were also careful, but ye lacked opportunity. [11]Not that I speak in respect of want: for I have learned, in whatsoever state I am, therewith to be content.

[12]I know both how to be abased, and I know how to abound: everywhere and in all things I am instructed both to be full and to be hungry, both to abound and to suffer need. [13]I can do all things through Christ, which strengtheneth me.

Paul knew how to be abased, in other words, he knew what it meant to be broke. He also knew how to abound; he knew what it meant to have financial prosperity flowing. Yet in both situations, he said he had learned to be content no matter what his finances looked like. The key to his ability to find contentment is the verse we love to quote so often, "I can do all things through Christ which strengtheneth me." We need to depend on the Lord completely in the area of our finances if we are to experience contentment.

Make Christ the focus of your life and He will give you His peace of mind. Jesus tells us in John 14:27, "Peace

I leave with you, my peace I give unto you: not as the world giveth, give I unto you. Let not your heart be troubled, neither let it be afraid." This type of peace is like someone bequeathing something to you in a will, the item belongs to you; all you have to do is accept the gift. Claim the peace that Christ has given to you.

Seek God first and He will meet every need in your life, including your financial needs. Matthew 6:33 says, "But seek ye first the kingdom of God, and his righteousness; and all these things shall be added unto you." The things that will be added to you in this verse are referring to natural things that we need such as clothing, food and shelter. We can claim God's promise to meet all of our needs as we keep Him first in our lives.

Pray About Financial Decisions

We should learn to pray about all purchases before we make them. I am convinced that if we had done this in the past, there are a whole lot of items that we never would have bought! Our God is a personal God who desires to lead us and teach us in our daily lives. God tells us in Proverbs 3:5, "Trust in the LORD with all thine heart; and lean not unto thine own understanding." In other words, we need to depend on God completely and not our own analysis of the situation. Sometimes we think too much!

Verse 6 says, "In all thy ways acknowledge him, and he shall direct thy paths." If we would just say, lead me Lord, He will willingly lead us to a place of blessing. When we are about to make a purchase, we need to step back from the situation and pray. Sometimes we just need to leave the mall, go home and pray. Developing this habit will keep us from impulsive shopping because God will tell us not to buy items that we don't need or that will be a strain on our budgets.

We need to also pray that the spirit of discipline that God has already given us will help us in managing our money. When we are disciplined, we set up our budget and stick with it. We spend money according to pre-determined limits and don't go overboard. We enjoy life more because now we can save for big goals such as buying a home, going on a nice vacation, college education for our children, or retirement.

II Timothy 1:7 in the NIV says, "For God did not give us a spirit of timidity, but a spirit of power, of love and of self-discipline." We already have discipline; we need to begin to use it!

Finally, we should pray for wisdom in the use of our finances. James 1:5 says, "If any of you lack wisdom, let him ask of God, that giveth to all men liberally, and upbraideth not; and it shall be given him." If you add up all the money a person makes in a lifetime, most people have a million dollars or more pass through their hands.

Sadly, the vast majority of people end up at retirement age with limited financial resources. Why? Because we lack wisdom in how to use the finances God has blessed us with. This book has attempted to destroy some of the ignorance people have regarding financial principles. However, it is only a starting point. God has a vast amount of wisdom that He is willing to freely share with us if we ask Him. Ask and you shall receive.

12

ETERNAL CONTENTMENT

Financial concerns may have been at the forefront of your mind prompting you to read this book. However, there are deeper issues of your heart that are far more important. Although this book has provided strategies to change both your attitude and actions regarding money, its Bible-based principles will be more effective if you have a relationship with the Lord Jesus Christ. The principles in this last short chapter are the most important of all and should be the first step in your journey towards financial victory.

Each one of us is born with a void deep within us. Many people spend a lifetime trying to satisfy that deep longing of the heart. We may try to fill that void with material things, money, education, career, status or relationships but ultimately none of those things will provide lasting fulfillment. Only Jesus Christ can fill that void within you.

If there has never been a time in your life when you have given your life to Jesus Christ, now is the time to do so. You may be a member of a church, however, God is not looking for a religious ritual; He is looking for a personal relationship. God has a specific plan for your life, but He can only speak to you and guide you if you have a relationship with Him.

Wherever you are right now, you need to recognize that you need God in your life. The Bible says in Romans 3:23, "For all have sinned, and come short of the glory of God." We have all made mistakes in our lives. But God has made a way for us to be in fellowship with Him. John 3:16 says, "For God so loved the world, that he gave his only begotten Son, that whosoever believeth in him should not perish, but have everlasting life."

To be saved, you just need to confess your faith in Jesus Christ through prayer. Romans 10:9-10 says, "That if thou shalt confess with thy mouth the Lord Jesus, and shalt believe in thine heart that God hath raised him from the dead, thou shalt be saved. For with the heart man believeth unto righteousness; and with the mouth confession is made unto salvation."

If you want to receive Jesus Christ as your Lord and Savior, then please pray the following prayer in faith.

> Dear God, I admit to you that I am a sinner and that I need you. Please forgive me for all the sins of my life. I believe that Jesus Christ is the Son of God and that He died on the cross for my sins and rose again on the third day. I receive you now Jesus as my Lord and Savior. I believe in my heart and I confess with my mouth that Jesus is Lord. Thank you God for saving me. By faith in your Word, I am now born again! In Jesus Name, Amen.

If you have prayed the above prayer in faith, you are now born again. Welcome to the family of God! Your next step after salvation is that you need to join a Bible-teaching church where your faith can be strengthened and you can grow in your relationship with God. Allow the Holy Spirit who now lives inside of you to teach you and guide you in everything you do.

ABOUT THE AUTHOR

DR. VICKY SPRING LOVE

God has anointed Dr. Vicky Spring Love as a powerful teacher of the Word, bringing change and wholeness to everyone she ministers to. Although she teaches on all aspects of Christianity, she has a particular anointing in the area of financial victory and is passionate about helping people get their finances in order so that their money can bring glory to God. She has ministered in the area of financial victory for over 25 years as a conference speaker, workshop leader and writer.

Dr. Vicky's first book, <u>Stop Robbing Peter to Pay Paul</u>, was selected as the textbook for the Finances and Stewardship class at Destiny School of Ministry, which has 34 locations worldwide. Her next book, <u>Changing Your Money Mindset</u>, is also being used as a textbook at the school.

Dr. Vicky co-authored another book, <u>101 Great Ways to Improve Your Life</u>, along with Jack Canfield (Chicken Soup for the Soul), John Gray (Men are from Mars, Women are from Venus), and Richard Carlson (Don't Sweat the Small Stuff). In addition, she has developed several other powerful, life-changing teaching CDs and ebooks.

Writing is a big part of Dr. Vicky's ministry. Her writings have appeared on www.streamingfaith.com, an online Christian television network featuring programming and editorials by other Christian ministers including Joyce Meyer, Bishop Eddie Long, and Dr. Myles Munroe. She has also been featured in The Detroit Free Press and on several television shows including "Live with Glenn

Plummer" on CTN, "Detroit Alive" and "Public Report" on TCT, and "The Alabaster Box".

Dr. Vicky is a licensed minister of the gospel and an associate minister at Family Victory Fellowship (FVF) in Southfield, Michigan under the leadership of Pastors Larry and Sylvia Jordan. At FVF, she is dean of the Ambassador Bible Training School, a two-year bible school affiliated with FVF.

An entrepreneur at heart, Dr. Vicky has owned several business ventures including a real estate investment firm, a residential mortgage company and a communications company. She earned a doctorate of Religious Education degree from Destiny Christian University, a Master of Business Administration degree in Finance from Oakland University and a Bachelor of Arts degree in Communications from the University of Detroit.

Although Dr. Vicky serves in many capacities, she feels her first ministry is at home. She and her husband, Glen, have enjoyed a wonderful marriage since 1981, and are the proud parents of two adult children.

OTHER RESOURCES FROM

DR. VICKY SPRING LOVE

Changing Your Money Mindset takes you through a journey that helps you to see how wrong thinking in the past has kept you stuck in the prison of a poverty mindset, how to increase your faith for prosperity and powerful techniques for transforming your mind in this area. Then in 21 short days, you will focus on a key strategy each day to literally change your money mindset to expect God's prosperity daily.
160 pages   **$18.00**

101 Great Ways to Improve Your Life - This dynamic book shows you how to achieve success in every area of your life – reaching goals, creating wealth, getting out of debt, and maintaining positive relationships. Co-authored with Jack Canfield (Chicken Soup for the Soul), John Gray (Men are from Mars, Women are from Venus), Richard Carlson (Don't Sweat the Small Stuff) and others.
396 pages   **$20.00**

Taking Authority Over Your Finances CD – Break every generational curse that is affecting your finances including a spirit of debt, lack, ignorance and settling for less than God's best for your life in this powerful, yet humorous, teaching! **$10.00**

Financial Crisis: The Cause & Our Response, 2 CD Set - With keen insight as a 15-year veteran of the mortgage industry, Vicky clearly explains what caused this crisis, how our nation has plunged from being under the blessing of God to being under a curse, and key strategies you can implement now. **$15.00**

Healing for Damaged Emotions CD Emotional hurts from the past may be still affecting you today, even causing physical illnesses. But Jesus Christ knows how you feel and is able to heal you emotionally. Be delivered today through the powerful anointing of the Spirit. **$10.00**

Honoring God with the Tithe CD Many people in the church today are not totally convinced that tithing is for today. They think that tithing is part of the law. Learn from the Word why tithing is for today and the blessings on tithers. If you don't tithe consistently, then you need to hear this! **$10.00**

165

Stop Robbing Peter To Pay Paul

ORDER FORM

To order any of our ministry resources, please log onto the websites, or complete the information below. Please make checks or money orders payable to and mail to:

Victory Jubilee Publishing,
P. O. Box 3286, Southfield, MI 48037

ITEM (Please List)	QUANTITY	TOTAL PRICE
SUBTOTAL:		
SHIPPING $2.50 for 1 item **FREE SHIPPING on 2 or more items shipped to US.** $5.95 international shipping		
TOTAL:		

INFORMATION ON YOU:

Name_____

Address_____

City_____ State_____ Zip Code_____

Telephone (____)_____

E-Mail Address:_____

Our Privacy Promise: We value your privacy and never sell or rent your personal information to any other company.